Horses, Bison & Beasts
of the Silk Routes

Horses, Bison & Beasts of the Silk Routes

Valentina DuBasky

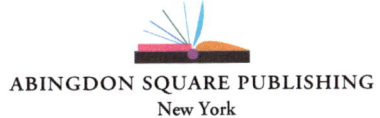

ABINGDON SQUARE PUBLISHING
New York

Copyright © 2024 by Valentina DuBasky

All rights reserved. No part of this publication may be reproduced in any manner, stored in a retrieval system, or transmitted in any form by any means—electronic, mechanical, photocopying, recording or otherwise—without written permission from the publisher, except in article reviews.

Artwork © 2024 by Valentina DuBasky

Horses, Bison & Beasts of the Silk Routes
published by
Abingdon Square Publishing
463 West Street, Suite G122
New York, NY 10014
USA
www.abingdonsquarepublishing.com
Book design: Abingdon Square Publishing

ISBN: 978-1-7349849-1-0
Library of Congress Control Number: 2024936754

Printed in the United States of America

Front Cover: *Spotted Cloud Horse,* 2018, acrylic and marble dust on plaster and paper, 29.75 x 32 inches,
Back Cover: *Spotted Goat with Spiral Horns,* 2017, oil on paper, 22 x 28 inches, and
Red Split Horse, 2016, oil on canvas, 22 x 30 inches

TABLE OF CONTENTS

Artist's Statement 1
Paintings 3
Watercolors & Monotype 39
CV 47
List of Plates 61

ARTIST'S STATEMENT

Bison, stags and horses are perennial subjects of my paintings. I am drawn to their rectangular shapes, their markings, and the structure of their horns and antlers. The paintings are created with thick impasto paint and incised markings, taking inspiration from my travels on the Silk Routes in China, India, Central and Southeast Asia, where I researched cave paintings and ancient art.

Over time, the bison, stag and horse paintings have evolved with changes in technique, materials, scale, and color, and include paintings in encaustic, paintings on plaster, and large monotypes with collage. During a trip to India, where I traveled to the Himalayas as a Fulbright Senior Specialist, and later visited the plains of Rajasthan, I was immersed in a world of spectacular colors out of which emerged a new palette for the horned and antlered animals. The colors include yellows of marigold, tints of coral, tangerine, crimson, and a range of blues, greens, violets, and all the compliments. The paintings celebrate the spiraling and coiling horns of goats, the lyre-shaped horns of bison, and the branching antlers of stags. In my paintings of horses, I adopted the colors of ancient art from the Silk Routes—madder, cinnabar, garnet, rose, indigo, amber, plum, ochre, and jade. A white bison in a red field from this series is wearing bells and was inspired the cattle that grazed near village temples in Cambodia.

The large quadrupeds that live in nature—and in the human imagination—are an endless source of inspiration. The energy of the animals evokes a world of mystery and possibility that inspires my paintings.

Valentina DuBasky
New York, NY, 2024

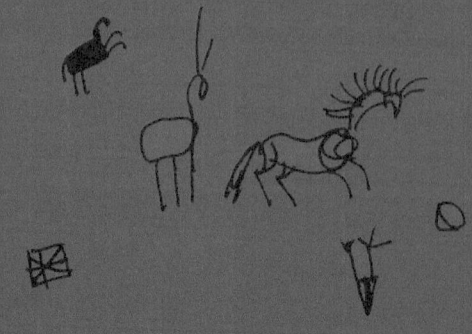

Paintings

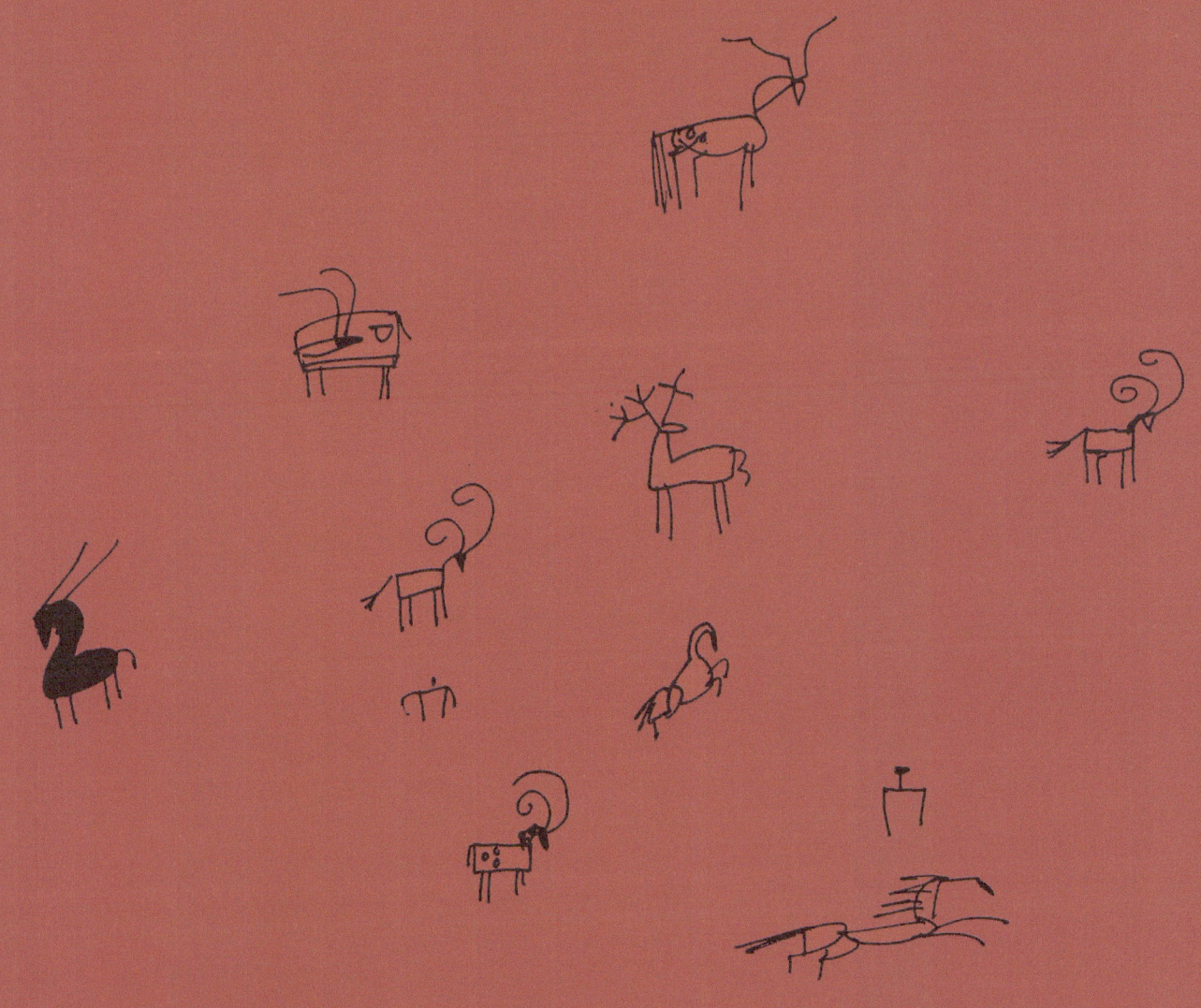

SPOTTED HORSE IN CLARET FIELD, 2016
Oil on canvas, 22 x 30 inches

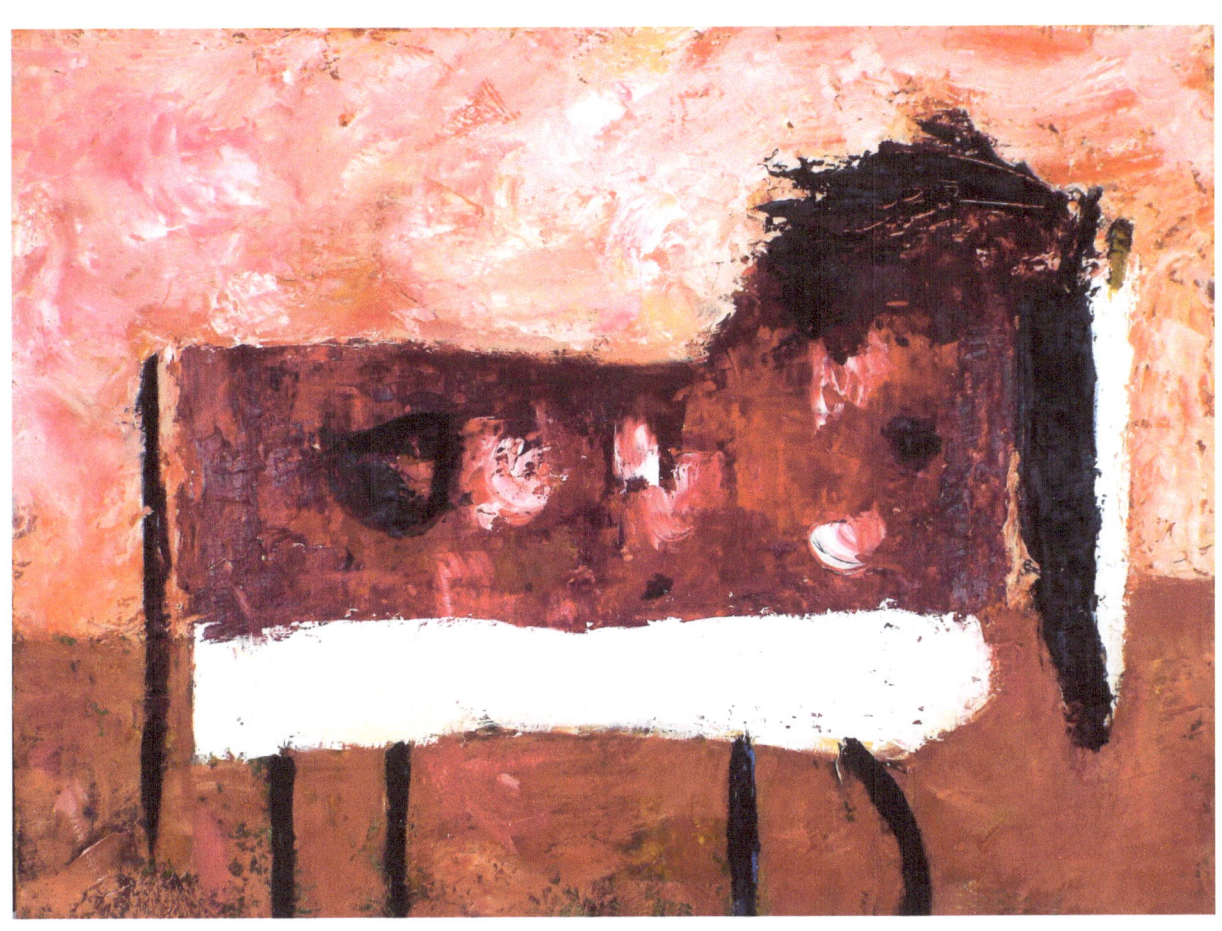

AMBER HORSE, 2016
Oil on canvas, 22 x 30 inches

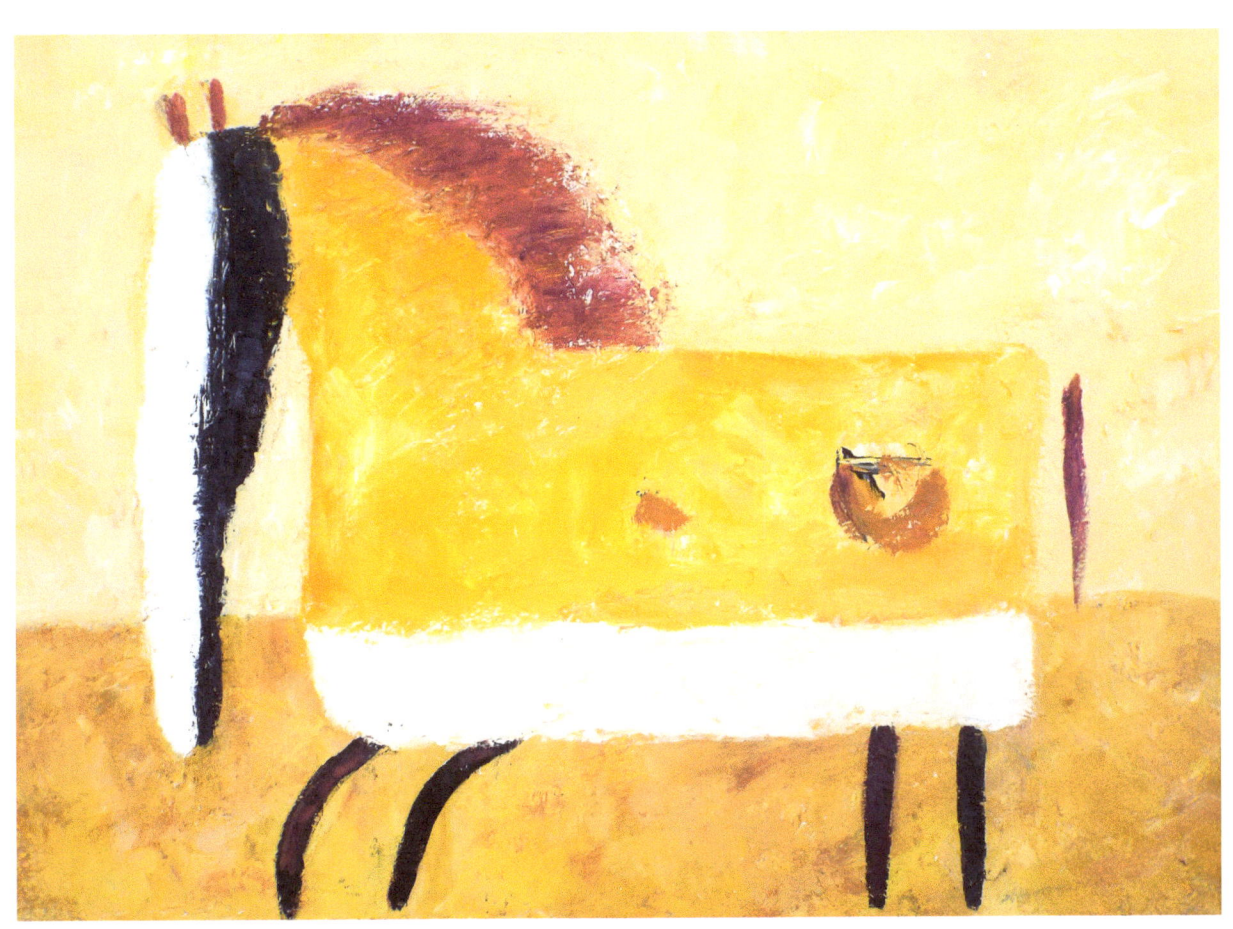

RED SPLIT HORSE, 2016
Oil on canvas, 22 x 30 inches

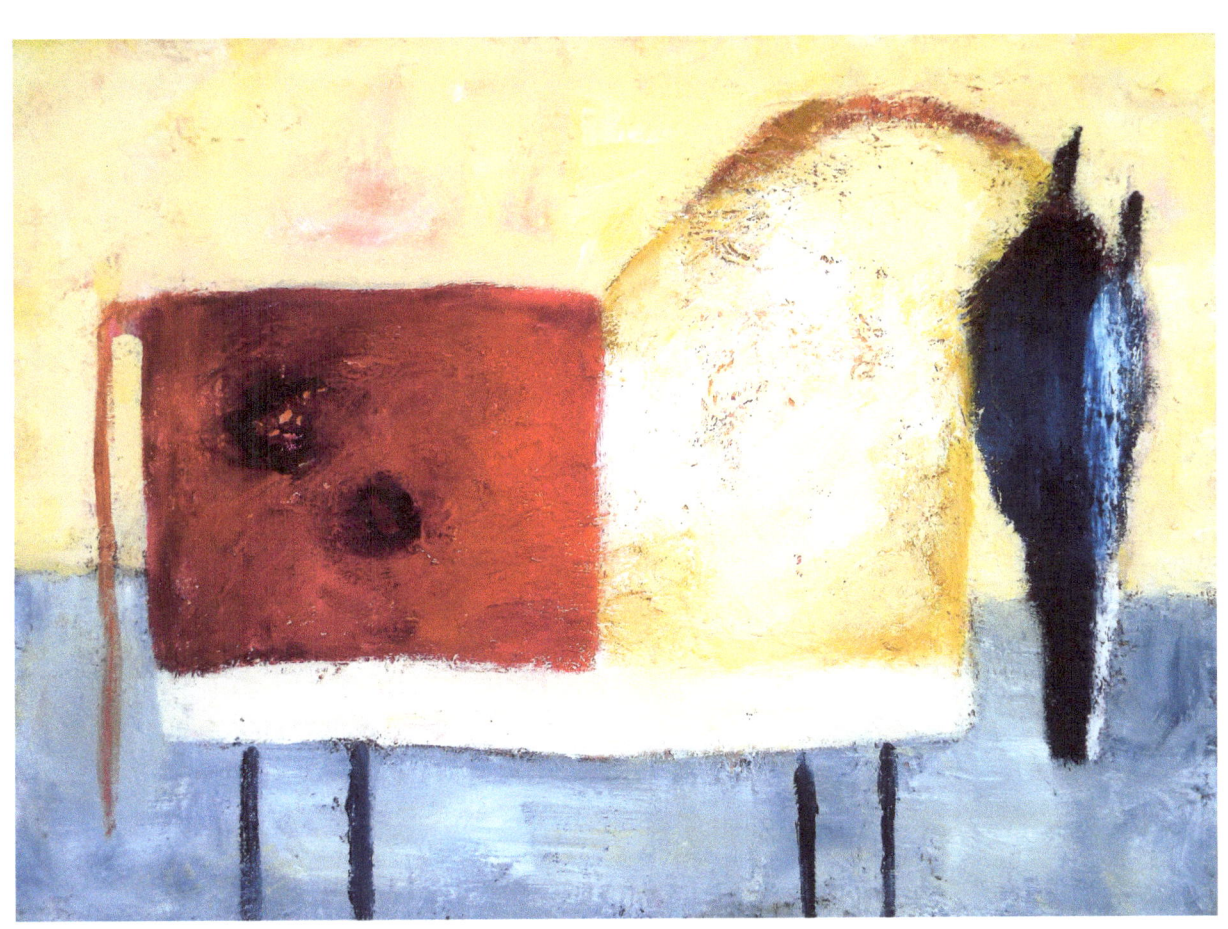

SPOTTED CLOUD HORSE, 2018
Acrylic and marble dust on plaster and paper, 29.75 x 32 inches

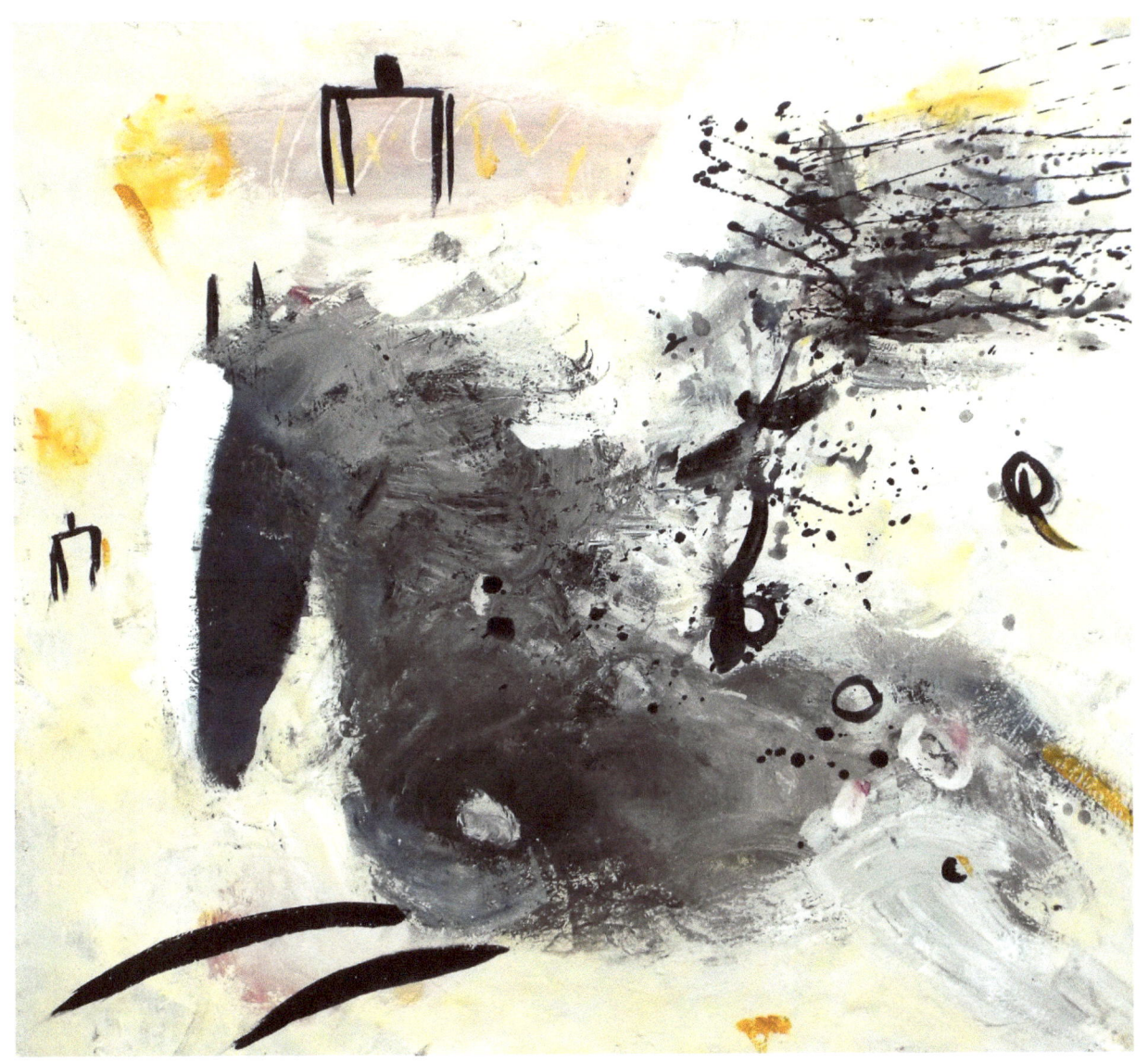

SPOTTED GOAT WITH SPIRAL HORNS, 2017
Oil on paper, 22 x 28 inches

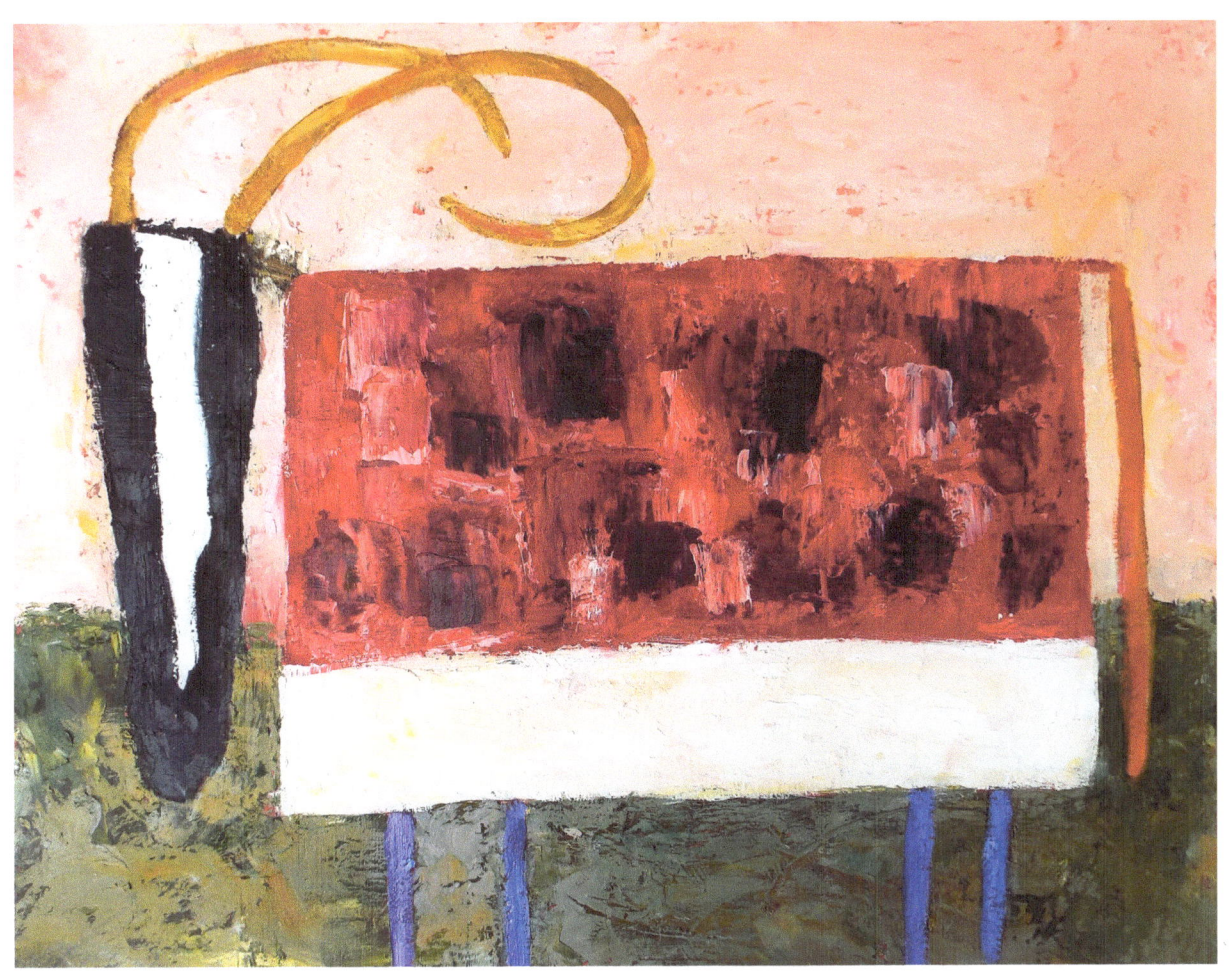

CERULEAN AND WHITE SPOTTED HORSE, 2017
Oil on paper, 22.5 x 30 inches

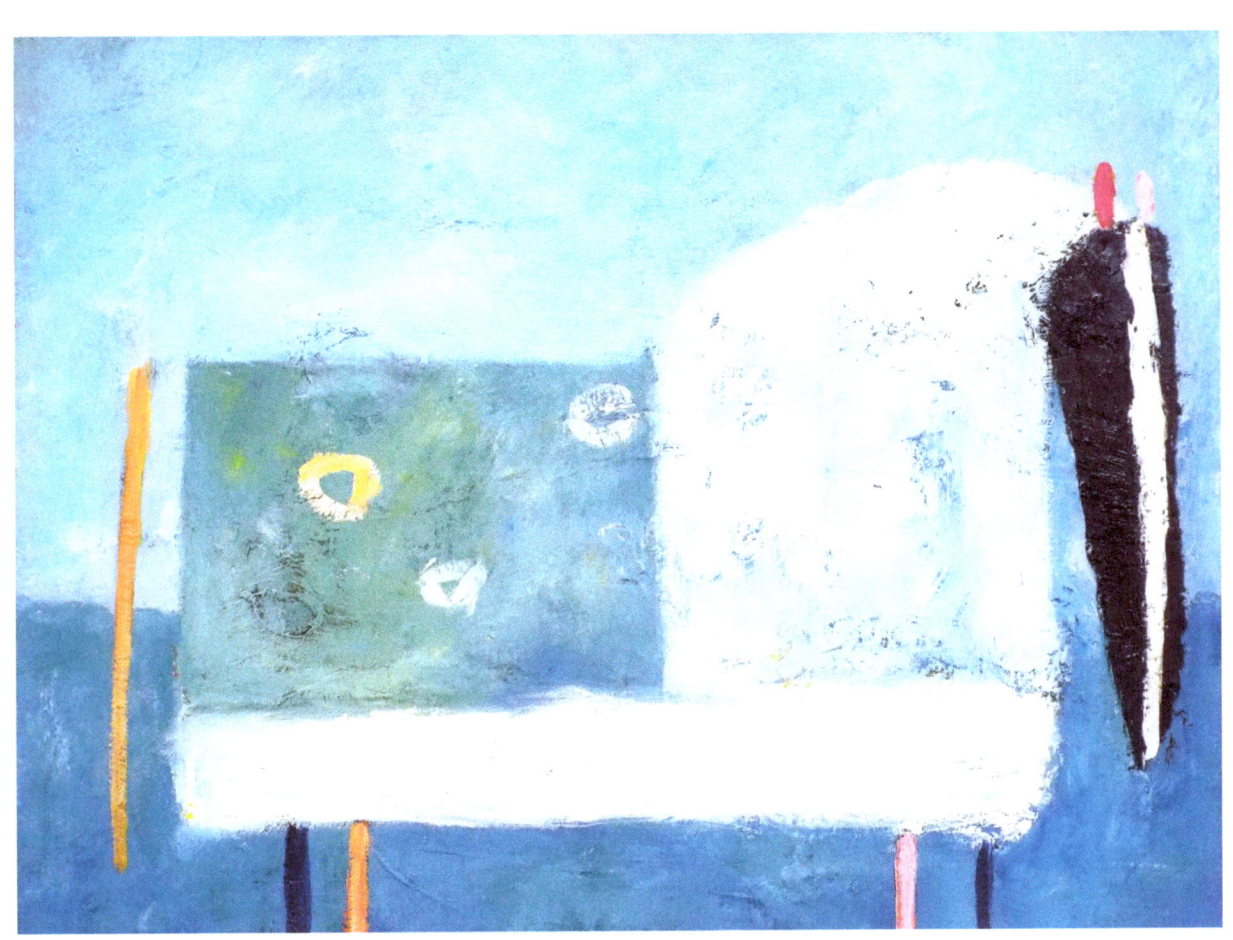

SPOTTED GOAT WITH AMBER HORNS, 2017
Oil on paper, 22 x 30 inches

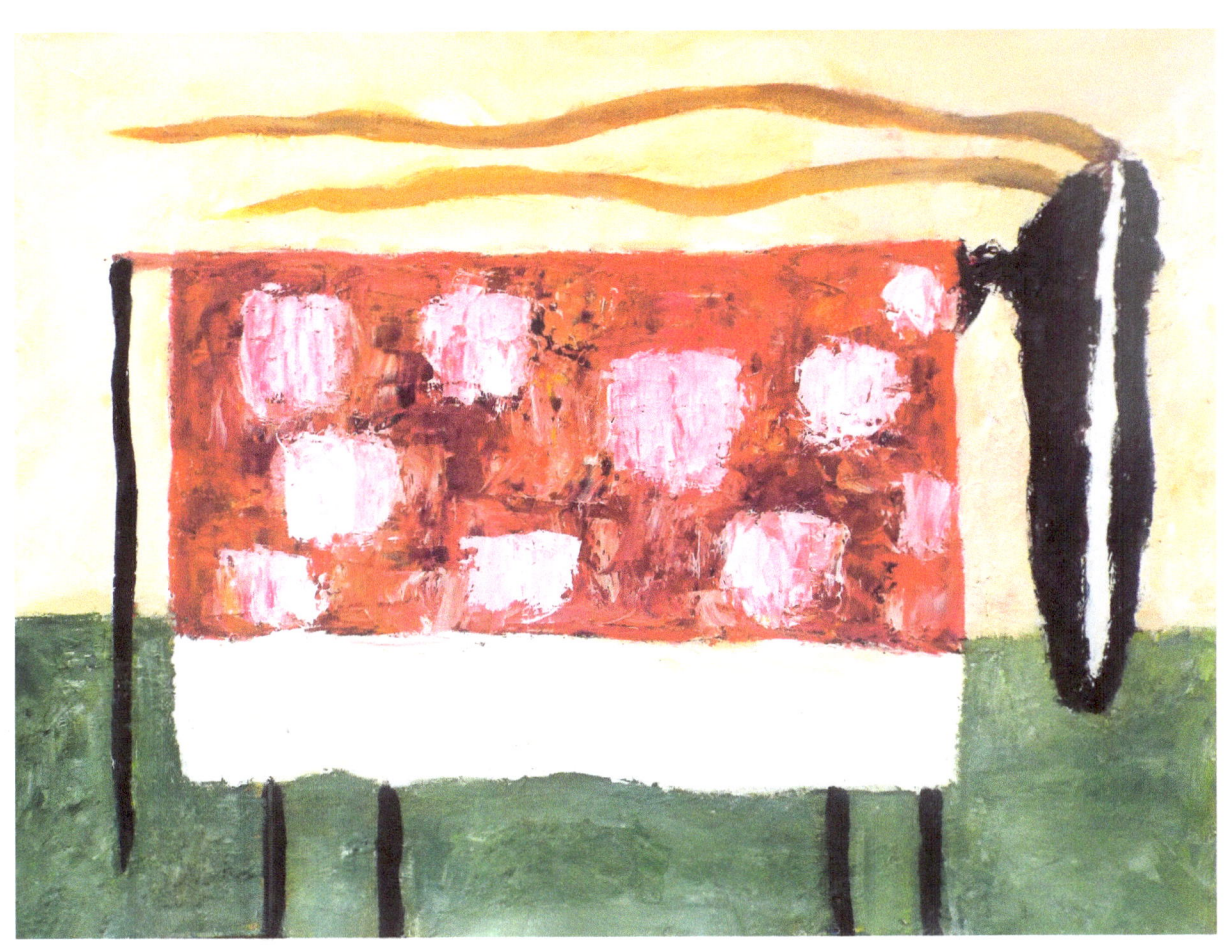

RED HORSE WITH BELLS, 2016
Oil on canvas, 22 x 30 inches

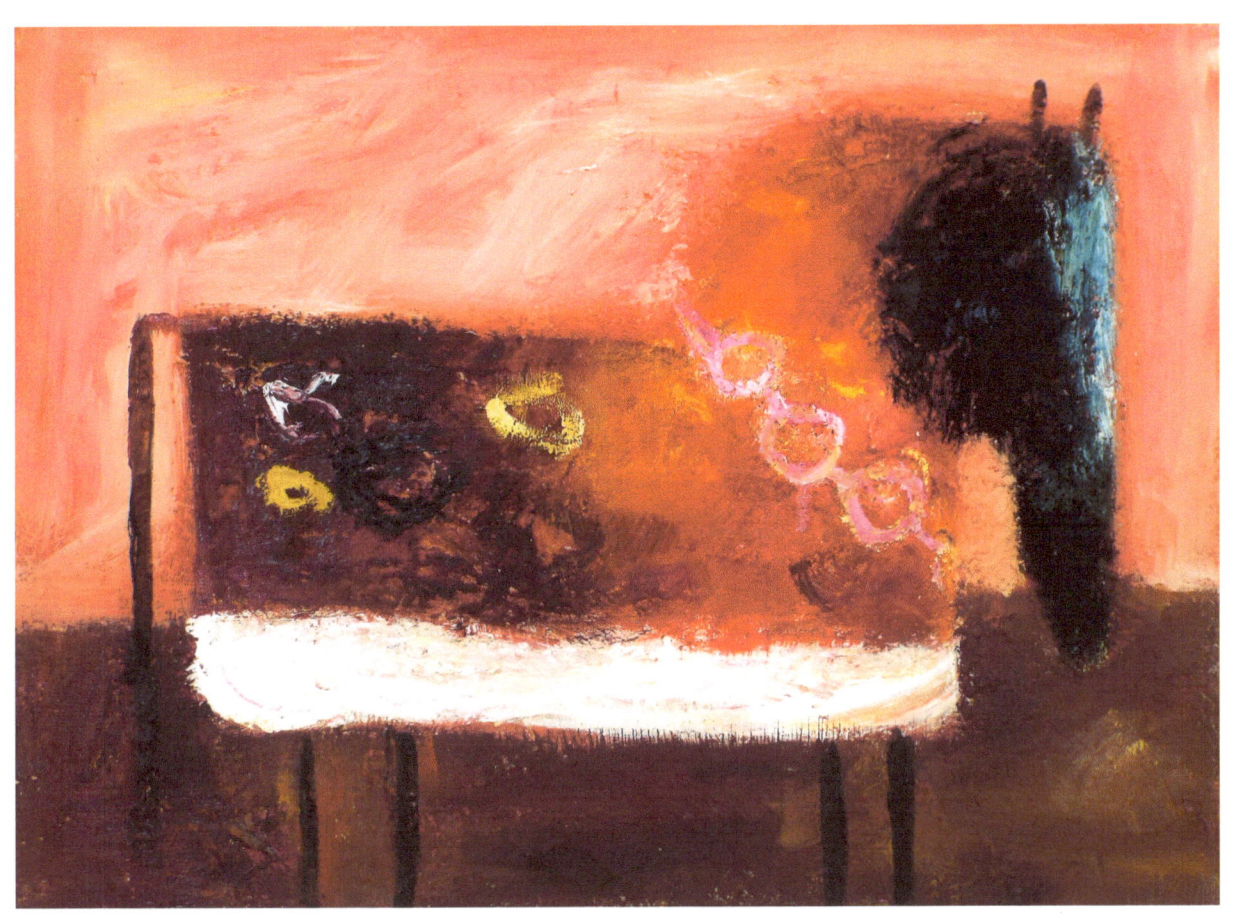

BISON, 2017
Mixed media on plaster and paper, 30.5 x 33 inches

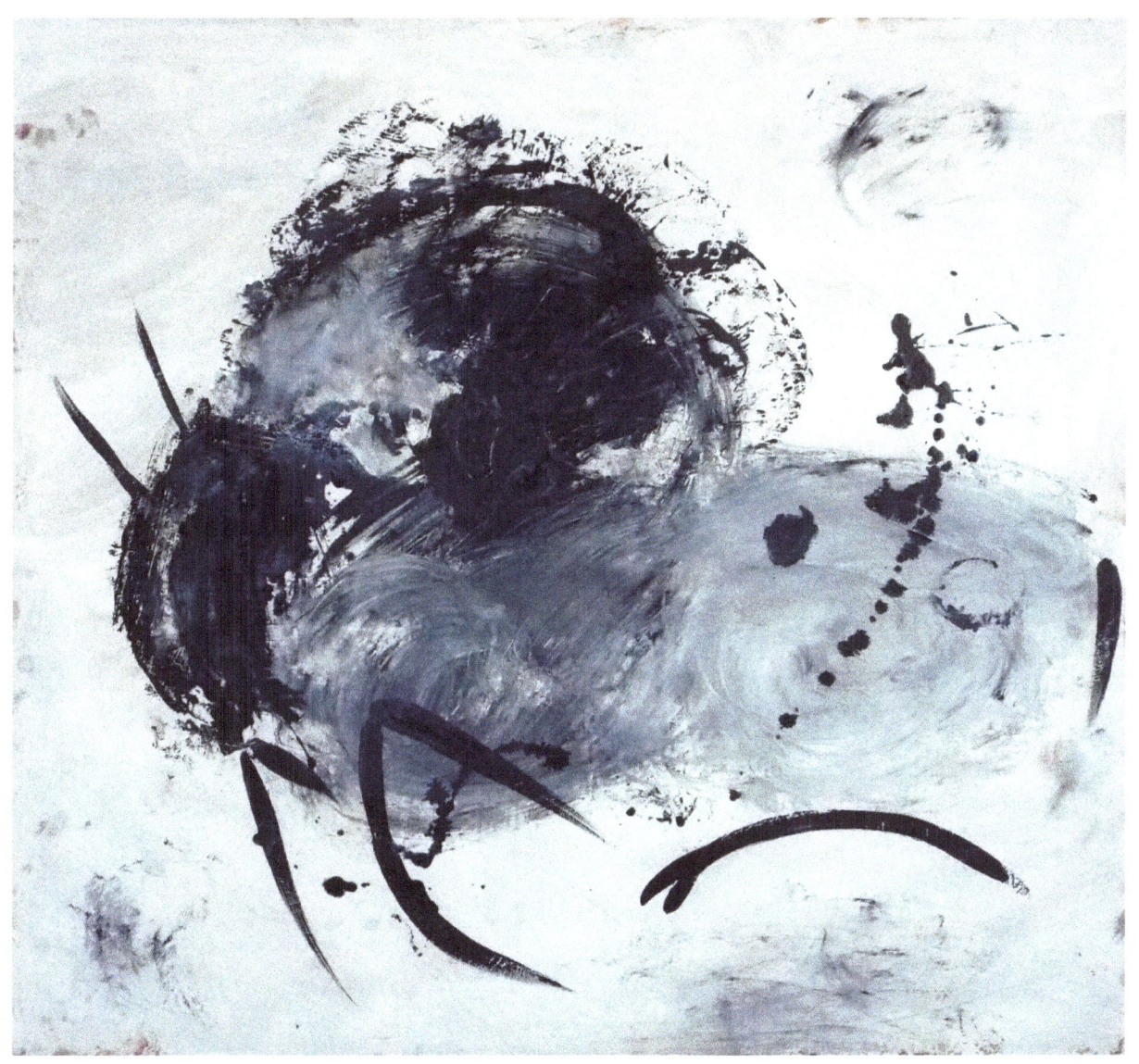

BLUE ANTLERED STAG IN RUST FIELD, 2017
Oil on paper, 22.5 x 30 inches

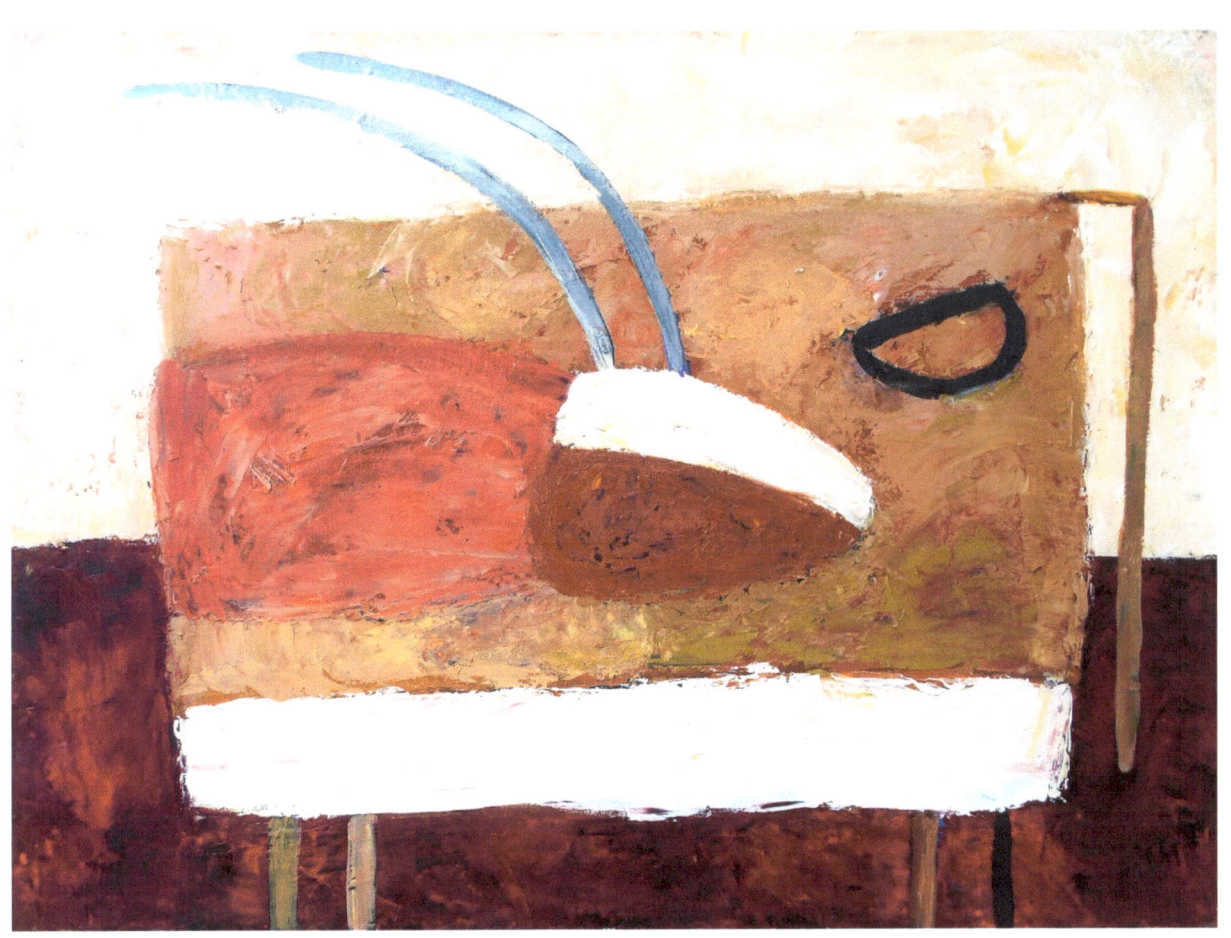

WHITE SPOTTED HORSE, 2017
Oil on paper, 22 x 30 inches

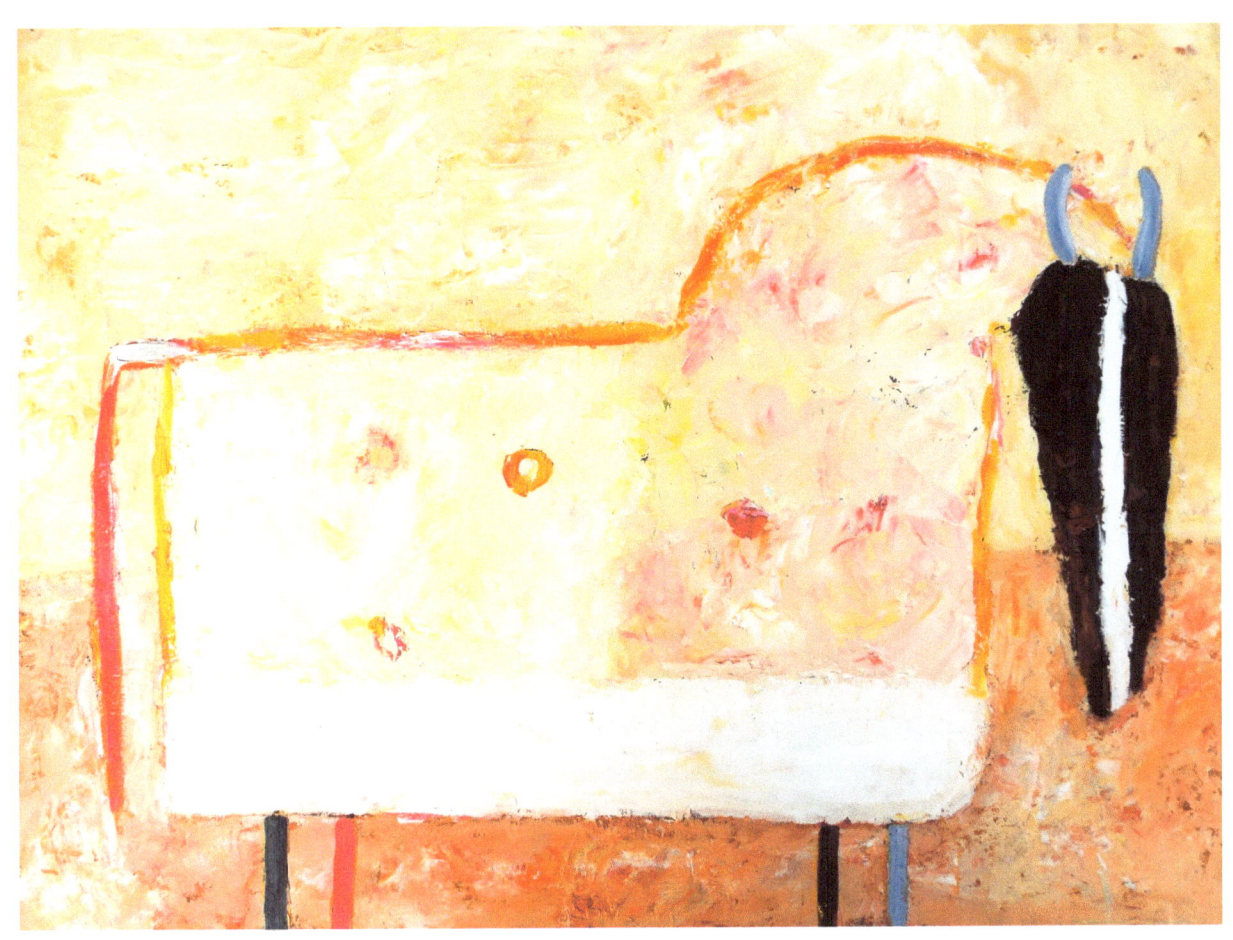

ANGKOR BISON IN ROSE FIELD, 2016
Oil on paper, 22 x 30 inches

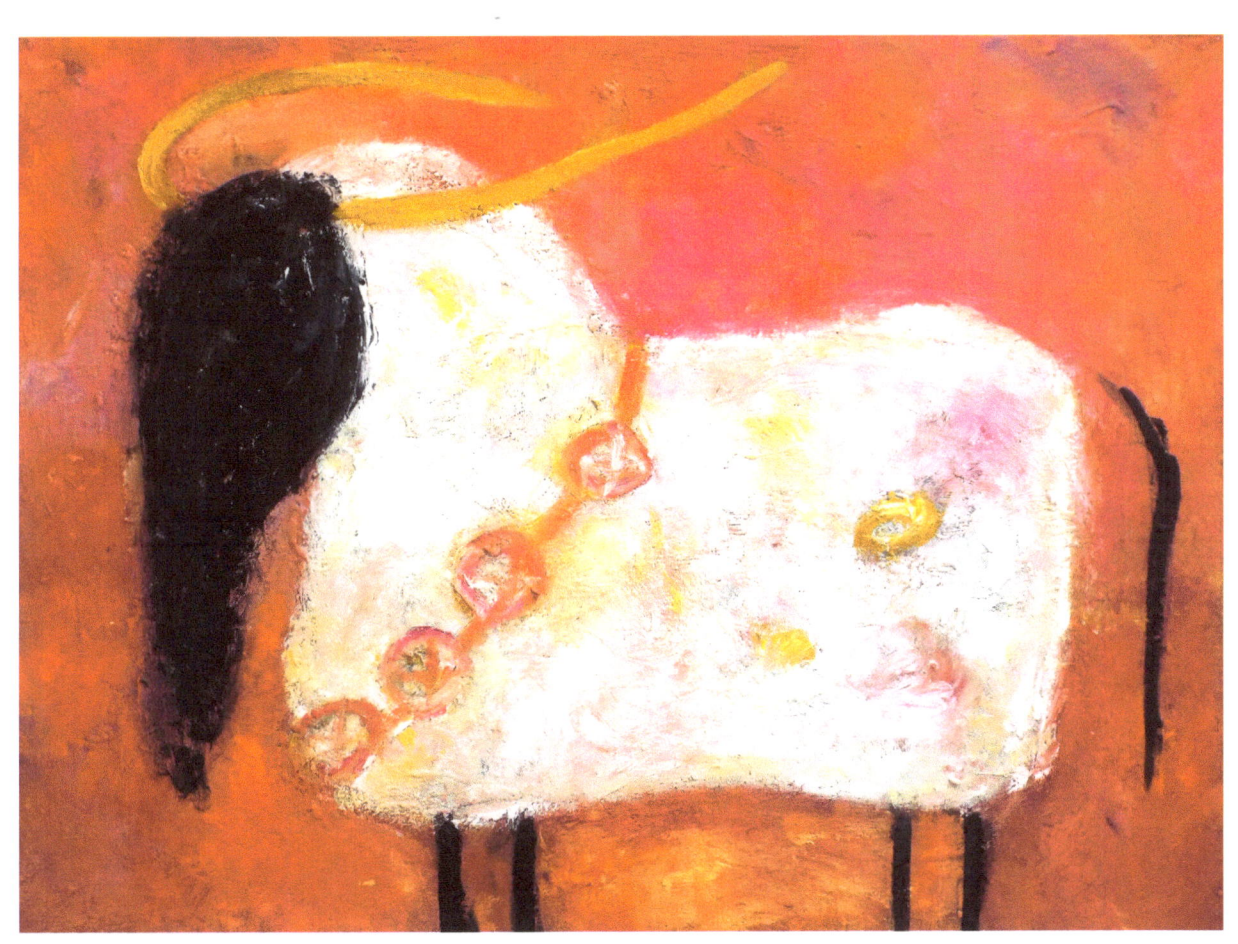

WINGED HORSE AND FIGURES, 2017
Mixed media on plaster and paper, 30.5 x 33 inches

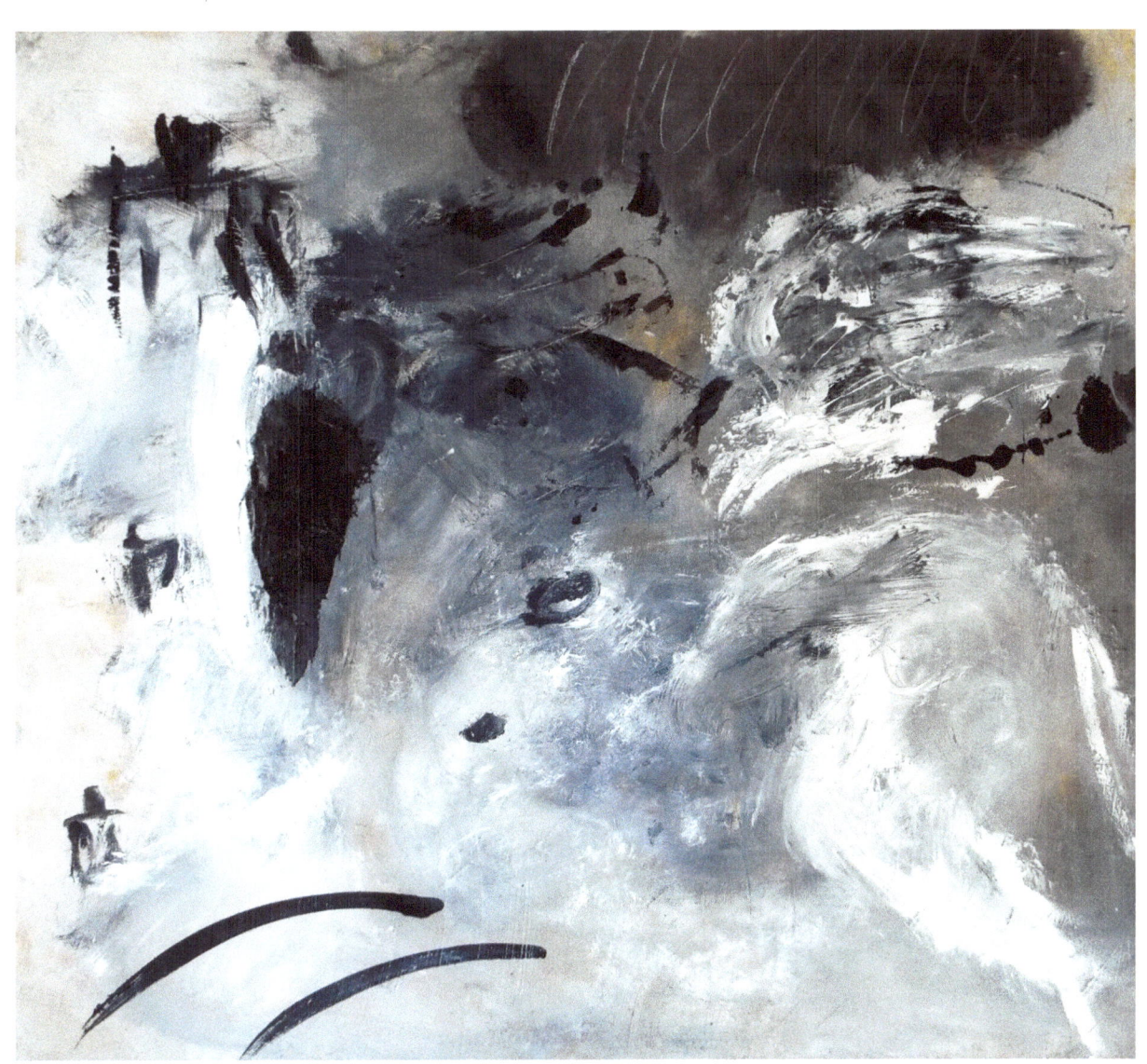

GREY SPOTTED HORSE IN PINK FIELD, 2017
Oil on canvas, 16 x 20 inches

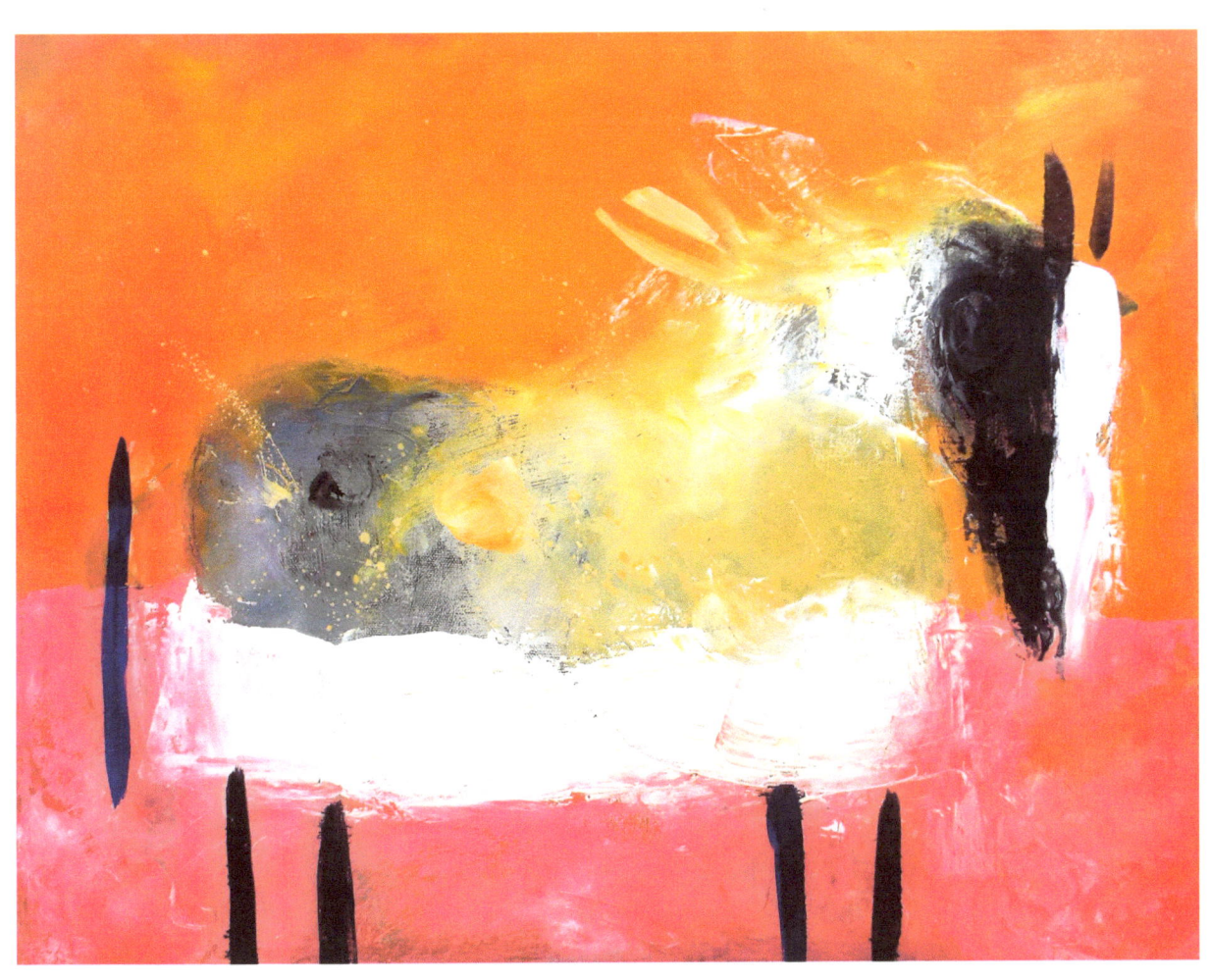

TURNING STAG WITH ROSE ANTLERS, 2020
Oil on paper, 22 x 30 inches

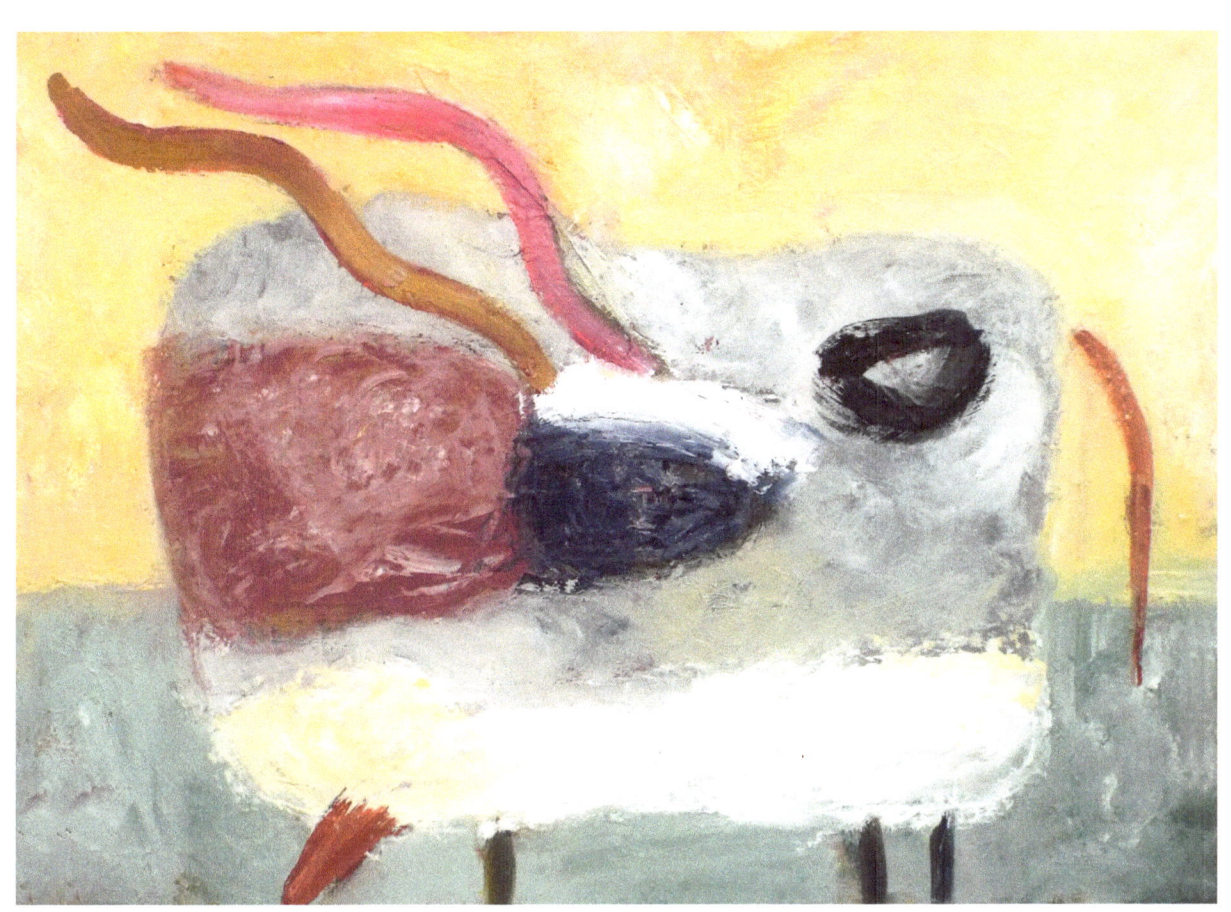

WINGED AMBER HORSE, 2018
Acrylic and marble dust on plaster and paper, 29.75 x 32 inches

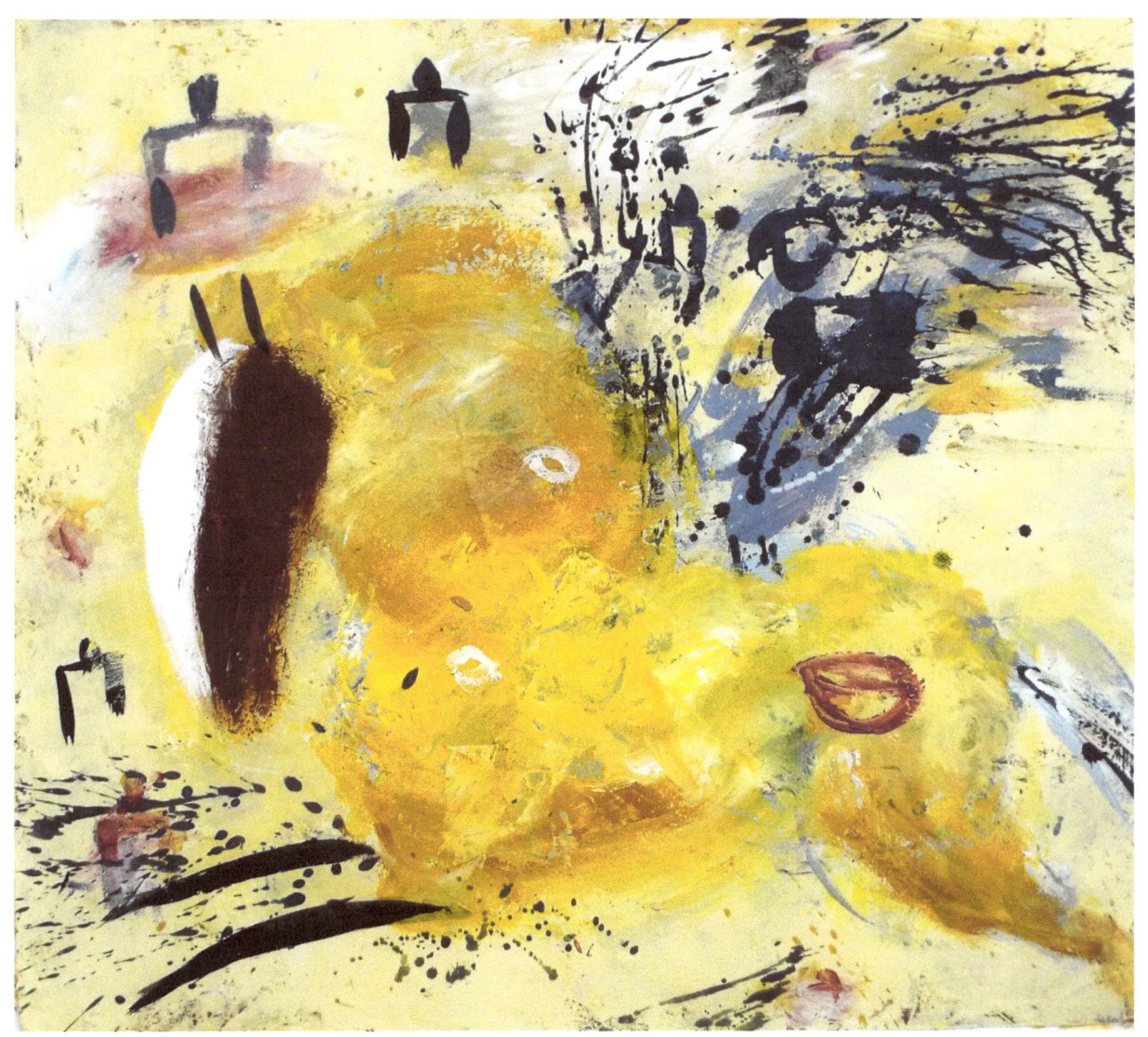

SPLIT STAG IN RED FIELD, 2018
Oil on canvas, 24 x 20 inches

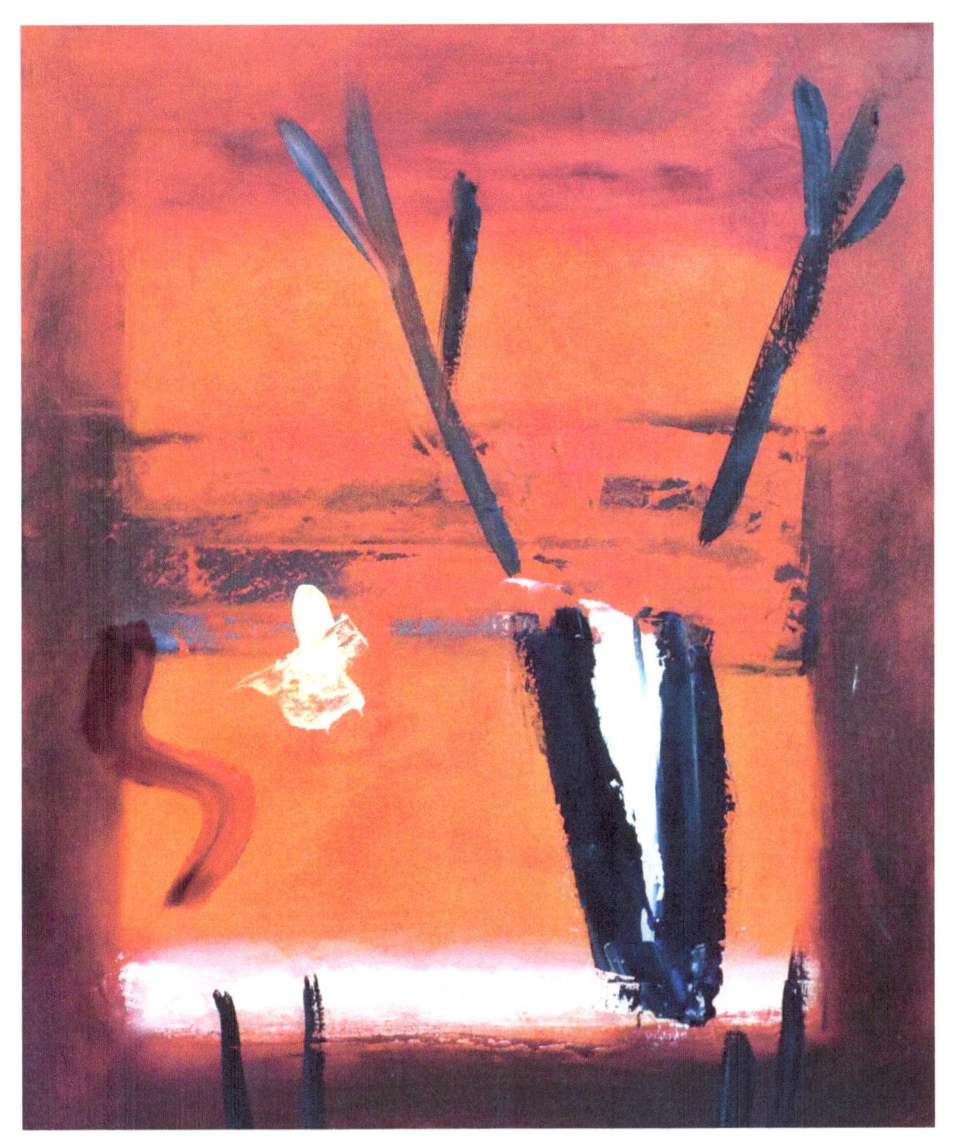

Watercolors & Monotype

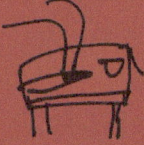

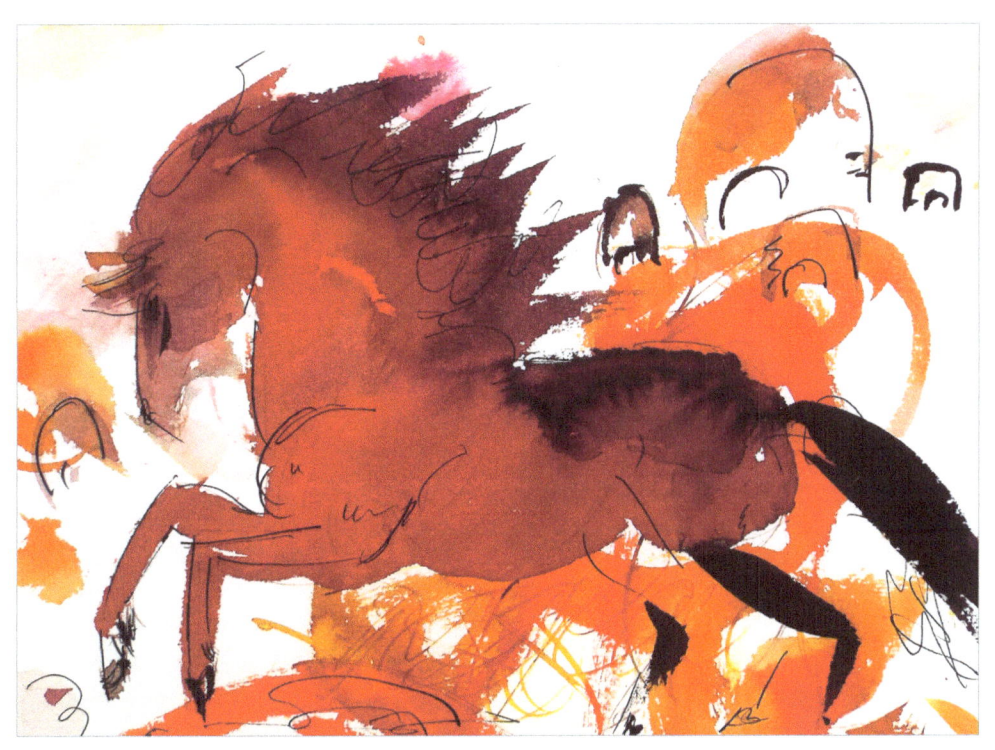

DUNHUANG HORSE, 2009
Watercolor and ink on paper, 6.25 x 8.75 inches

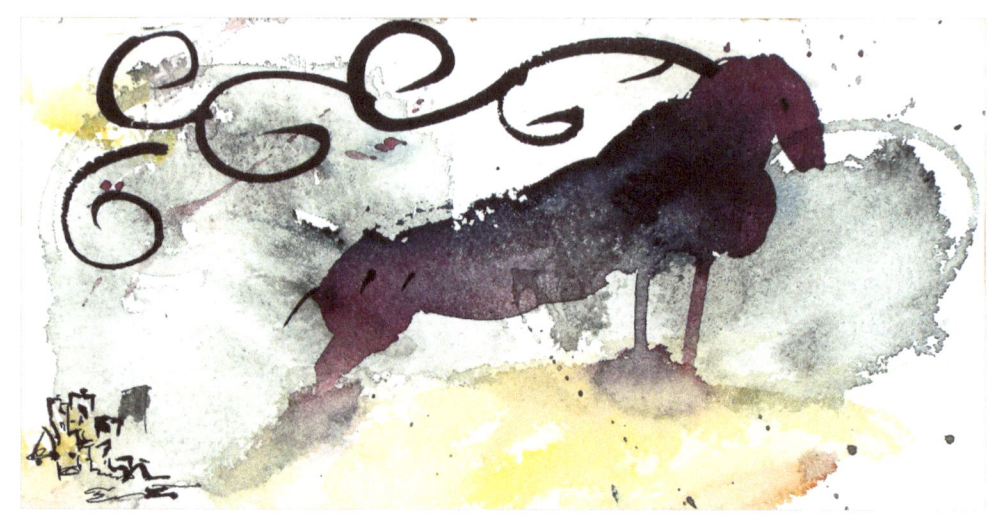

MARKHOR GOAT WITH SPIRAL HORNS, 2009
Watercolor and ink on paper, 4.5 x 9 inches

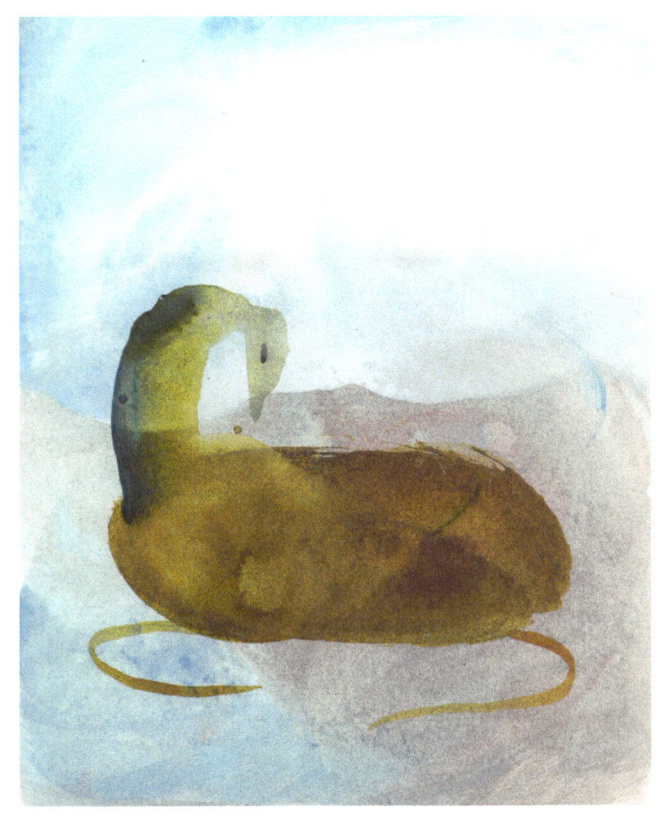

RECUMBENT HORSE WITH TURNING HEAD, 2014
Watercolor monotype with gouache, 12 x 9 inches

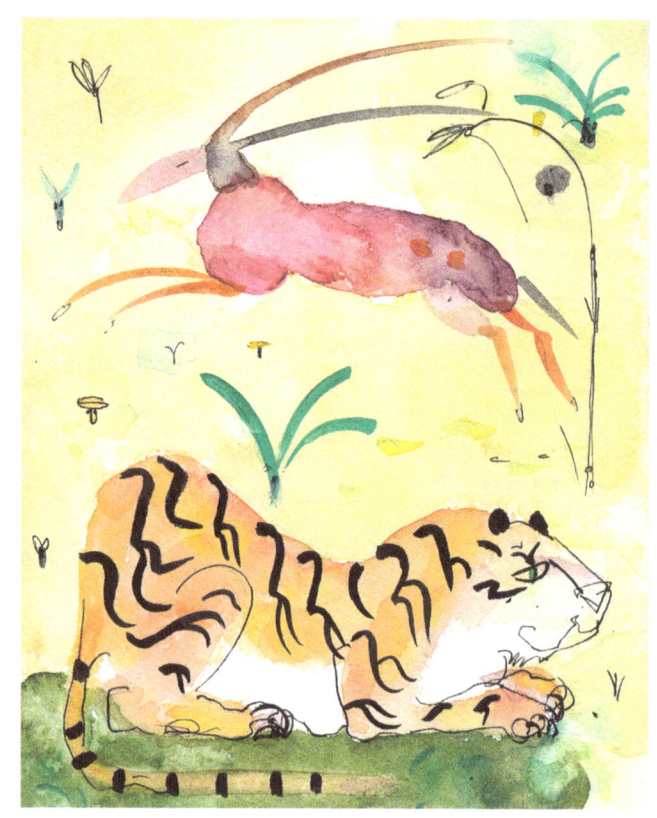

LEAPING DEER AND TIGER, 2009
Watercolor and ink on paper, 8.75 x 7 inches

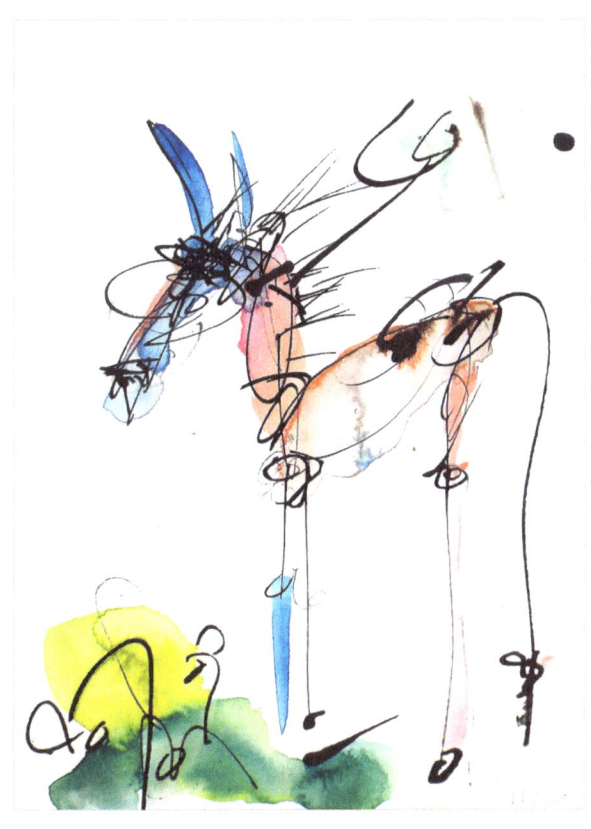

DONKEY, 2009
Watercolor and ink on paper, 7.5 x 5.5 inches

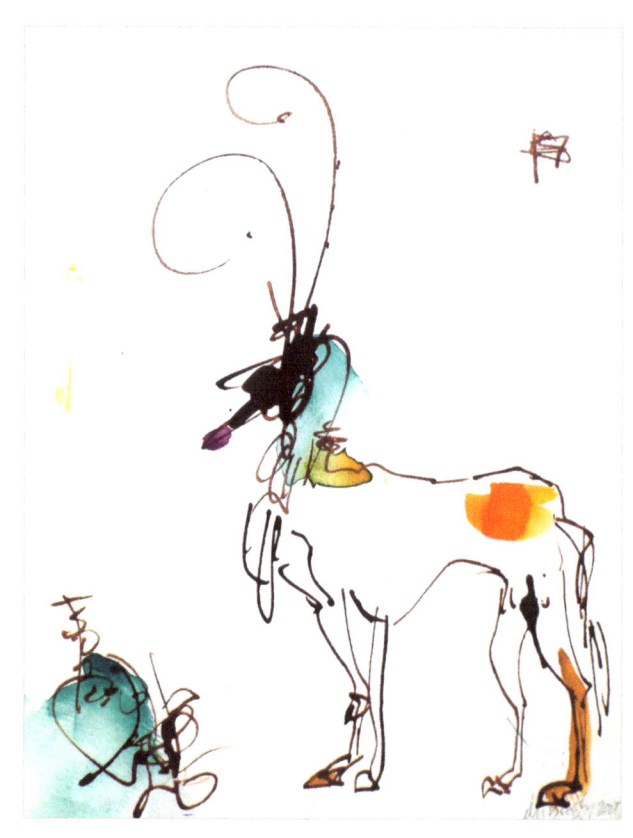

GOAT, 2009
Watercolor and ink on paper, 7.5 x 5.5 inches

ONE-PERSON EXHIBITIONS

2024	"Birds of the Silk Routes", Abingdon Square Viewing Room, online exhibition
	"Horses, Bison & Beasts of the Silk Routes", Abingdon Square Viewing Room, online exhibition
2020	"Horned & Antlered Animals", Abingdon Square Viewing Room, online exhibition, New York, NY
2008	"Mongolian Horses and Siberian Tigers", Cheryl Pelavin Fine Arts, New York, NY
	"Cambodian Flower Archaeology Monotypes", Cheryl Pelavin Fine Arts, New York, NY
2006	"Review: Cranes, Herons and Waterbirds", Cheryl Pelavin Fine Arts, New York, NY
	"Preview: Rainforests, Cloudforests and Pine", Cheryl Pelavin Fine Arts, New York, NY
	"Paintings", College of the Marshall Islands, Majuro, Republic of the Marshall Islands
2005	"The Crane Series", Ogilvie-Pertl Gallery, Chicago, IL
	"Riverbirds & Rainforests", The National Academies of Sciences, Washington, DC
	"Materia Medica", The Creative Center, New York, NY
2004	"The Crane & Heron Series", Cheryl Pelavin Fine Arts, New York, NY
	"Paintings by Valentina DuBasky", Friesen Fine Arts, Sun Valley, ID
	"Atlantic Flyway Project", Teaneck Creek Conservancy, Teaneck, NJ
2002	"New Paintings", Hodges Taylor Gallery, Charlotte, NC
	"New Paintings", Friesen Fine Arts, Sun Valley, ID
2001	"New Paintings", Silpakorn University Art Center Gallery, Bangkok, Thailand
	"Orchids and Fossils: New Landscape Paintings", Cheryl Pelavin Fine Arts, New York, NY
2000	"Ancient Futures: New Paintings & Monoprints", Cheryl Pelavin Fine Arts, New York, NY
	"Representation Debut," Friesen Fine Arts, Seattle, WA
	"Orchids on the Way to the Temple", Galerie Timothy Tew, Atlanta, GA
	"Through Bending Trees", Friesen Fine Arts, Sun Valley, ID
1998	"Memory and Light: New Paintings", Cheryl Pelavin Fine Arts, New York, NY
	"Materia Medica: New Monoprints", Cheryl Pelavin Fine Arts, New York, NY
1997	"Paintings", Hodges Taylor Gallery, Charlotte, NC
	"Landscape, Archaeology & Memory, Paintings, Sculpture & Monoprints 1985-97", University of North Carolina Gallery, Asheville, NC
1995	"Painting Retrospective", Rena Haveson Gallery, Pittsburgh, PA
	"Photographs", Gallery f32, Asheville, NC
1991	"New Paintings", Ruth Siegel Gallery, New York, NY
1990	"New Paintings", Ruth Siegel Gallery, New York, NY
1987	"Bronze Sculpture from the Caravan Series", Empire Bronze Art Gallery, LIC, NY
1986	"Paintings on Paper", Oscarsson-Siegeltuch Gallery, New York, NY
	"Paintings & Monotypes", Hodges Banks Gallery, Seattle, WA
1985	"Recent Paintings", van Straaten Gallery, Chicago, IL
	"Recent Paintings", Oscarsson Hood Gallery, New York, NY
	"Paintings from the Stag Series", Gloria Luria Gallery, Miami, FL
	"Monotypes", Jay Gallery, New York, NY
1984	"Recent Paintings", Susan Montazenos Gallery, Philadelphia, PA

1983	"Paintings from the Stag Series", Oscarsson Hood Gallery, New York, NY
	"Recent Paintings", Robert L. Kidd Gallery, Detroit, MI
1981	"Paintings on Paper", Oscarsson Hood Gallery, New York, NY
1980	"Paintings", Semaphore Gallery, New York, NY

SELECTED GROUP EXHIBITIONS

2020	"Monoprint 2020 - Printers and Presses", Washington Art Association & Gallery, Washington Depot, CT
2019	"The Black and White Show", 11 Jane St. Art Center, Saugerties, NY
2018	"United States Embassy Exhibition", Art in Embassies Program, United States Embassy, Beijing, China
	"Collective Memory", Equity Gallery, New York, NY
2017	"The Trace", Lichtundfire Gallery, New York, NY
2015	"Small Works", Carter Burden Gallery, New York, NY
	"True Monotypes", International Print Center New York, curated by Janice Oresman, New York, NY
	"Group Exhibition", McElwain Fine Arts, St Louis, MO
2014	"Shifting Ecologies", The Painting Center, New York, NY
	"Tandem Press Monoprints", Expo Chicago, Chicago, IL
	"Tandem Press Monoprints", IFPDA Print Fair, New York Armory, New York, NY
	"Tandem Press Monoprints", NYINK Art Fair, Miami Beach, FL
2013	"Tandem Press Monoprints", IFPDA Print Fair, New York Armory, New York, NY
	"Tandem Press Monoprints", NYINK Art Fair, Miami Beach, FL
2010	"Spring Prints", Cheryl Pelavin Fine Arts, New York, NY
2009	"Paintings", Friesen Fine Arts, Seattle, WA
	"Streetscapes", Landscapes, Still Lives, Jan Larsen Art, New York, NY
	"Art and Democracy", Gallery H, New York, NY
2008	"Friends", Cheryl Pelavin Fine Arts, New York, NY
	"From Different Horizons of Rock Shelter", Pang Mapha Archaeological Site, Thailand
	"From Different Horizons of Rock Shelter", National Gallery of Art, Bangkok, Thailand
	"Print Show", Cheryl Pelavin Fine Arts, New York, NY
2007	"25 Years of Printmaking at Cheryl Pelavin Fine Arts", Cheryl Pelavin Fine Arts, New York, NY
2006	"Alignment", Friesen Fine Art, Seattle, WA
	"Oil & Wax", Robert Roman Galleries, Scottsdale, AZ
	"Group Show", Ogilvie-Pertl Gallery, Chicago, IL
	"Art Scottsdale", Ogilvie-Pertl Gallery & Larsen Gallery, Scottsdale, AZ
	"Traveling Exhibition: Agent Orange: Consequence of War, a Call to Conscience", Marlboro College Gallery, Vermont; Brandeis University Gallery, Boston; George Washington University Gallery, Washington, DC
2005	"Oil & Wax: Chapter & Verse", Siano Gallery, Philadelphia, PA
2004	"Two Artists", Ogilvie-Pertl Gallery, Chicago, IL
	"Dealer's Choice", Robert L. Kidd Gallery, Detroit, MI

	"The New Realism", Robert L. Kidd Gallery, Detroit, MI
	"Two Artists: Reflections of Cambodia", The Puffin Foundation, Teaneck, NJ
	"Returning the Brownfields of Teaneck Creek", Teaneck Creek Conservancy, Teaneck, NJ
	"Toxic Landscape", Long Beach Island Foundation of the Arts & Sciences, Love Ladies, NJ
	"Lower Manhattan Cultural Council Benefit", DKNY, New York, NY
2003	"Flora and Fauna: Manifestations", Cheryl Pelavin Fine Arts, New York, NY
	"American Artists", United States Embassy, Panama City, Panama
2002	"American Artists", United States Embassy, Riga, Latvia
	"American Artists", United States Embassy, Tallinn, Estonia
	"Two Artists", Friesen Fine Art, Seattle, WA
	"Fifteenth Anniversary Exhibition", Galerie Timothy Tew, Atlanta, GA
	"Affordable Art Fair", Cheryl Pelavin Fine Arts, New York, NY
	"The Head Show", Galerie Timothy Tew, Atlanta, GA
	"Reactions", Exit Art, New York, NY
	"Toxic Landscape: Artists Look at the Environment", Bibliotéca Nacional José Martí, Havana, Cuba
2001	"Group Exhibition", Friesen Fine Art, Seattle, WA
	"Group Exhibition", Norton Gallery, Seattle, WA
	"World Trade Center Benefit Exhibition", Cheryl Pelavin Fine Arts, New York, NY
2000	"Group Exhibition", Friesen Fine Art, Sun Valley, ID
1999	"American Artists", United States Embassy, Lima, Peru
	"American Artists", United States Embassy, Reykjavik, Iceland
	"American Artists", United States Embassy, Bangkok, Thailand
	"Sitting Pretty", Met Life Windows, New York, NY
	"Birdsong", Laurie Seeman Gallery, Nyack, NY
1998	"Visual Dialogues: 15 Women Artists", Robert Kidd Gallery, Detroit, MI
	"Nature/Culture", The New York Arts Exchange Show, New York, NY
	"Four Artists", Lone Star Park Gallery, Dallas, TX
	"Group Exhibition", Tower Air, curated by Jeannie Greenberg, New York, NY
1997	"Sizzle", Jeffrey Coploff Gallery, New York, NY
	"Group Exhibition", Hillwood Museum, Chattanooga, TN
	"Art of Hearts", Nora Haime Gallery & the National Academy of Design, New York, NY
	"Group Exhibition", Hodges Taylor Gallery, Charlotte, NC
	"The National Horse Show", Robert Kidd Gallery, Detroit, MI
1996	"Partners in Printmaking: Works from Solo Impressions", National Museum of Women in the Arts, Washington, DC
	"Painting Exhibition", Hillwood Museum, Long Island University, NY
	"Three Photographers", June Kelly Gallery, New York, NY
	"American Artists", United States Embassy, Muscat, Oman
	"Recent Monotype Editions", Pelavin Editions, New York, NY
	"Group Exhibition", Robert L. Kidd Gallery, Detroit, MI

1995	"American Artists", United States Embassy, Amman, Jordan
	"Inaugural Exhibition", Michele Bigue Gallery, Fort Lauderdale, FL
1994	"American Artists", United States Embassy, Oslo, Norway
	"Group Exhibition", ES Painting Space, New York, NY
1993	"Animal Imagery", Champion Paper, curated by Janice Oresman, Hartfield, CT
1992	"34 Raumes", Documenta, Berlin, Germany
	"Printmaking from the Permanent Collection", Jane Voorhees Zimmerli Art Museum, Rutgers University, NJ
	"Works on Paper from Pelavin Editions", The Armory Show, New York, NY
1991	"Works on Paper", Champion Paper, Stanford, CT
1990	"Intaglio Printing in the 1980's", Jane Voorhees Zimmerli Art Museum, Rutgers University, New Brunswick, NJ
	"Women in Print", Traveling museum exhibition, National Museum of Women in the Arts, Washington, DC
	"Menagerie", General Electric Company Headquarters, curated by MOMA Advisory Services, CT
1989	"Surface Printing in the 1980's", Jane Voorhees Zimmerli Art Museum, Rutgers University, NJ
	"Creatures", Benson Gallery, Bridgehampton, NY
1988	"Three Sculptors Working in Bronze", Gallerie Helene Grubair, Miami, FL
1987	"Group Show", Albright Knox Museum, Buffalo, NY
1986	"Monotypes by Gallery Artists", Oscarsson-Siegeltuch Gallery, New York, NY
	"Paintings", van Straaten Gallery, Chicago, IL
	"Inaugural Exhibition", Group Show, Oscarsson-Siegeltuch Gallery, New York, NY
	"Homage to Ana Mendieta", Zeus Trabia Gallery, New York, NY
	"Monotypes", Jay Gallery, New York, NY
1985	"Art of the 70's & 80's", Aldrich Museum of Contemporary Art, Ridgefield, CT
	"1985 Invitational Quinquennial Exhibition", Oscarsson Hood Gallery, New York, NY
	"Selections from the Jane Voorhees Zimmerli Art Museum", The Grolier Club, New York, NY
	"Chicago Art Expo", Oscarsson Hood Gallery, Chicago, IL
	"Pelavin Editions 1985", Jay Gallery, New York, NY
	"Monotypes and Works on Paper", Robert L. Kidd Gallery, Detroit, MI
	"Animals: Contemporary Visions", Robert L. Kidd Gallery, Detroit, MI
	"The Animal Within", Jay Gallery, New York, NY
	"Young Printmakers", Roger Ramsey Gallery, Chicago, IL
	"Two Artists", Peri Renneth Gallery, West Hampton, NY
1984	"Painting Invitational", Robeson Center Gallery, Rutgers University, New Brunswick, NJ
	"Situations", Jamaica Arts Center, The Newark Museum Collection, Newark, NJ
	"Review/Preview", Oscarsson Hood Gallery, New York, NY
	"Works on Paper", Wolff Gallery, New York, NY
	"8 at 84", Robert Feldman Gallery, New York, NY
	"Works on Paper", Barbara Greene Gallery, Miami, FL
	"Ringing in the New", Jay Gallery, New York, NY

1983   "New Acquisitions", Newark Museum, Newark, NJ
"Art on Paper", Weatherspoon Museum, Greensboro, NC
"Group Exhibition", Oscarsson Hood Gallery, New York, NY
"Works on Paper", Frumpkin Struve Gallery, Chicago, IL
"Group Show", Albright Knox Museum, Buffalo, NY

1982   "Group Show", Albright Knox Museum, Buffalo, NY
"New Acquisitions", Alternative Museum, New York, NY
"Mixed Bag", Alternative Museum, New York, NY
"Group Exhibition", McNay Art Institute, Collectors Gallery VI, Austin, TX
"Works on Paper", Roger Ramsey Gallery, Chicago, IL
"Group Exhibition", Oscarsson Hood Gallery, New York, NY

1981   "New Acquisitions", Aldrich Museum of Contemporary Art, CT
"Nine Artists Invited", Meisal Gallery, New York, NY
"Group Exhibition", Semaphore Gallery, New York, NY
"The Working Process", O.I.A. Exhibition, New York, NY
"Group Exhibition", Newcomber Westreich Gallery, Washington, DC

1980   "Small Works", 80 Gallery, Washington Square East, New York, NY
"Group Show," Race Gallery, Philadelphia, PA
"4 Artists", Soho Center for Visual Artists, New York, NY
"Betty Parsons at Robert L. Kidd Gallery", Robert L. Kidd Gallery, Detroit, MI

COLLECTIONS

MUSEUM COLLECTIONS

Alternative Museum, New York, NY
Herbert F. Johnson Museum, Cornell University, Ithaca, NY
National Museum of Women in the Arts, Washington, DC
Newark Museum, Newark, NJ
Orlando Museum of Art, Orlando, FL
Seattle Art Museum, Seattle, WA
Jane Voorhees Zimmerli Art Museum, Rutgers, NJ
Xianghai Museum, Xianghai Nature Reserve, Xianghai, China

LIBRARY COLLECTIONS

Library of Congress (Exit Art Reactions Exhibition), Washington, DC
New York Public Library, Lionel Pincus and Princess Firyal Map Division, New York, NY

SELECTED PUBLIC COLLECTIONS

Agrace Hospice Care, Madison, WI
Architectural Arts, Inc, Dallas, TX
Banca della Suizzeria Italiana, NY, NY
Bank Boston, Boston, MA
Barron & Budd, NY, NY
Chase Manhattan Bank, NY, NY
Chemical Bank, NY, NY
Citibank International, Miami, FL
Denrich Leasing Company, Miami, FL
Echo Lab, MN
Carey Ellis Company, MN
Ernst & Young, NY, NY
Evergreen Asset & Management Corporation, NY, NY
Federal Reserve Bank, Chicago, IL
First National Bank, Boston, MA
Fuzhou International Center, Fuzhou, China
General Instruments, NY, NY
General Mills, Inc, Minneapolis, MN
Goldman-Sachs, NY, NY
Gruntal, NY, NY
Henson & Effron, St. Paul, MN
Hospital Corporation of North America, Nashville, TN
IBM Collection, Los Angeles, CA
Indiana National Bank, Boston, TX
International Data Group, Boston, MA
Kempner Insurance Company, NY, NY
King Investment Advisor, Inc, Houston, TX
Lang Communications, NY, NY
Sidney Lewis Collection, Richmond, VA
Martin Margulies Collection, Miami, FL
Mayo Clinic, Rochester, MN
McDonalds Corporation, Oak Brook, IL
The Mercer Company, NY, NY
J. P. Morgan & Company, NY, NY
Morgan Guarantee, NY, NY
Nutter, McClennan & Fish, Boston, MA
Palm Hills Hotel, Okinawa, Japan
Peat, Marwich, Mitchell & Co, Montvale, NJ

Pew Charitable Trust, Philadelphia, Pa
Pfizer Pharmaceuticals, Inc, NY, NY
Polsinelli Collection, Los Angeles, CA
Prudential Life Insurance Company, Rockefeller Center, NY, NY
Quad Graphics, West Allis, IL
Quaker Oats, Chicago, IL
Randolph & Tate Associates, NY, NY
Reich & Tang, NY, NY
Simpson, Thacher, Bartlett, NY, NY
Skadden, Arps, Slate, Meagher & Flom, NY, NY
Solomon Equities, Inc, NY, NY
Tower Air, NY, NY
United States Department of State, Washington, DC
Vinson Elkins, Houston, TX
Wachovia, Charlotte, NC
E.M. Warburg Pincus, NY, NY
WFAE National Public Radio, Charlotte, NC
C. Wright Design, Mill Valley, CA
Zale Corporation, Dallas, TX
Zelle & Larson, St. Paul, MNWachovia, Charlotte, NC
E.M. Warburg Pincus, New York, NY
WFAE National Public Radio, Charlotte, NC
C. Wright Design, Mill Valley, CA
Zale Corporation, Dallas, TX
Zelle & Larson, St. Paul, MN

GRANTS

2016   Fulbright Specialist Program, India
2006   Visiting Artist Grant, Pang Mapha Highland Archaeology Project, Thailand
2003   Earthwork Installation Grant, Atlantic Flyway Project, Teaneck Creek Conservancy
2002   American Artists Abroad, Art in Ambassies Program Grant, US Department of State, Riga, Latvia
        American Artists Abroad, Art in Ambassies Program Grant, US Department of State, Tallinn, Estonia
        The Puffin Foundation Grant, paintings and photographs
2001   United States Embassy Visiting Artist Grant, Bangkok, Thailand
1999   Pollock Krasner Foundation
1986   Pollock Krasner Foundation
1984   Ariana Foundation for the Arts

PRESS

PUBLIC TELEVISION

2005   Goodman, Janice; Feature, **WETA Public Television**, Around Town, Best Bets, August 5; one-person exhibition at the National Academy of Sciences Gallery, Washington, DC

REVIEWS OF ONE-PERSON EXHIBITIONS

2008   "Mongolian Horses and Siberian Tigers- New Paintings on Paper and Canvas" **Absolutearts.com: Indepth Art News,** October 23; Review of one-person exhibition at Cheryl Pelavin Fine Arts, NYC; Color reproduction: *Crouching Tiger,* 2008

2007   Vachon, Michelle; "Back to Basics: Two Artists' Return to Drawing" **The Cambodia Daily**, Issue 483, June; Review of one-person exhibition at Java Cafe Gallery, Phnom Penh; Color reproductions: *Crossing the Street in Hanoi,* 1994 and *Resting Soldier,* 1994

Ledden, Liz; "Cambodian Journal: Human resilience and the strong Cambodian spirit are themes that artist Valentina DuBasky explores in her new exhibition", **Asia Life**; Review of one-person exhibition at Java Cafe Gallery, Phnom Penh

2006   Schwendener Martha; Review, **The New Yorker**, April 17; Review of one-person exhibition at Cheryl Pelavin Fine Arts, NYC

2005   LaFaso, Vanessa; "Larger Than Life: DuBasky's Oversize Work Focuses on Animal, Plant Life Along Silk Road", **The Washington Diplomat,** October; Review of one person exhibition at the National Academy of Sciences Gallery, Washington, DC; Color reproductions: *Gray Bird and Branches,* 2005, *Riverbirds, Fossils and Reeds,* 2005 and *Mountain Site,* 2003

Tierney, Robin; Review, **The Examiner**, October 29; Review of one-person exhibition at the National Academy of Sciences Gallery, Washington, DC; Color reproduction: *Red Bird & Reeds,* 2005

2002   **State Magazine,** "In the News: Artist and Their Art Go Abroad" No. 46. December, 2002, p5 Color Reproduction: *Heron, Warbler and Milkweed,* 1991

2001   Wilkinson, Jeanne C.; Review, **Tribeca Tribune,** Vol. 8, No. 4, December; Review of one-person exhibition at Cheryl Pelavin Fine Arts, NYC; Color reproduction: *Forest Site Wat Phimai,* 2001

"Ancient Futures: Cave-wall Landscape Paintings" **Bangkok Post**, June, 22; Review of one-person exhibition at Silpakorn Gallery, Silpakorn University, Bangkok, Thailand; Color reproduction: *Forest Site with Orchids & Bending Trees,* 2000

Review, **Naew Na**, June; Review of one-person exhibition at Silpakorn Gallery, Silpakorn University, Bangkok, Thailand

2000	Johnson, Ken; Review, **The New York Times**, February 4; Review of one-person exhibition at Cheryl Pelavin Fine Arts, NYC
	Silverstein, Joel; Review, **Review Magazine**, January; Review of one-person exhibition at Cheryl Pelavin Fine Arts, NYC
	Review, **Idaho Mountain Express,** Arts & Events, Sun Valley, Idaho, August 2; Review of one-person exhibition at Andria Friesen Fine Arts, Seattle; Color reproduction: *Forest Site with Spotted Stag*, 2000
	"New and Old", **The Nation,** July; Review of one-person exhibition at Silpakorn Gallery, Silpakorn University, Bangkok, Thailand; Color reproduction: *Forest Site with Orchids & Bending Trees*, 2000
	Review, **Siam Rath,** June 21; Review of one-person exhibition at Silpakorn Gallery, Silpakorn University, Bangkok, Thailand
	"Ancient Futures", **Bangkok Post;** Review of one-person exhibition at Silpakorn Gallery, Silpakorn University, Bangkok, Thailand; Color reproductions: *Forest Site with Orchids & Bending Trees,* 2000 and *Forest Floor with Orchids*, 2000
	"Ancient Futures: Cave-wall Landscape Paintings"; **Bangkok Post;** Review of one-person exhibition at Silpakorn Gallery, Silpakorn University, Bangkok, Thailand; Color reproduction: *Forest Site with Stag & Bird*, 2000
1999	Henry, Gerrit; Review, **Art in America,** January; Review of one-person exhibition at Cheryl Pelavin Fine Arts, NYC; Color reproduction: *Syntax*, 1998
1997	Grau, Jane; Review, **Charlotte Newsstand,** Arts & Entertainment, November 1; Review of one-person exhibition at Hodges Taylor Gallery, Charlotte; Color reproduction: *Red Spotted Horse*, 1997
1991	Cohen, Ronny; Review, **Artforum,** December; Review of one-person exhibition at Ruth Siegel Gallery, NYC; Color reproduction: *Indonesia*, 1991
1986	Henry, Gerrit; Review, **Art in America,** April; Review of one-person exhibition at Oscarsson-Hood Gallery, NYC; Reproduction: *Primate*, 1986
	Broelley, Doen; "Modern Day Cave Painting", **The Weekly,** Vol. 11, No. 25, June 18; Review of one-person exhibition at Hodges Banks Gallery, Seattle; Color reproduction: *Sienna Stag, 1984*
1985	Review, **Gallery Guide,** December; Review of one-person exhibition at Oscarsson Hood Gallery, NYC; Reproduction: *Rough Beast, 1984*
	Shanks, John Arthur; "Prehistory to Post Modernism", **Women Artists News,** Vol. 9, No. 2, Winter; Review of one-person exhibition at Semaphore Gallery, NYC; Reproduction: *Fallow Deer in Bracken,* 1983
	Harper, Paula; Review, **Miami News,** Miami Art Scene, April; One-person exhibition at Gloria Luria Gallery, Miami
1983	Zimmer, William; Review, **Arts Magazine;** Review of one-person exhibition at Oscarsson-Hood Gallery, NYC; Color reproduction: *Amber Stag*, 1983

1981   Parks, Addison; Review, **Arts Magazine,** Vol. 55, No. 6; Review of one-person exhibition at Semaphore Gallery, NYC; Color reproduction: *Split Cow,* 1981

Pellicone, William; Review, **Artspeak**, Vol. 2, No. 9; Review of one-person exhibition at Semaphore Gallery, NYC; Reproduction: S*plit Cow,* 1981

Shanks, John Arthur; Review, **Women Artists News,** Winter/Spring; One-person exhibition at Semaphore Gallery, NYC; Color reproduction: *Split Cow,* 1981

FEATURE ARTICLES

2006   "Rain Clouds: Valentina DuBasky at Cheryl Pelavin Fine Arts", **The New York Sun**, On The Town, May 18; Color reproduction: *Riverbank Late Afternoon,* 2006

2003   Gomez, Edward M.; "Reimagining the Landscape: Contemporary Painters Bring Fresh Ideas and Techniques to a Classic Art Form", **Art & Antiques,** Vol. 26, No. 10, October; Color reproduction: *Open Forest,* 2001

Cebere, Gundega; "Amerikas Maksla Riga", **Maksla Plus: Kulturas Zurnals,**Vol. 1, No. 33, February/March; Color reproductions: *Heron,* 1995, and *Heron, Warbler and Milkweed,* 1991

Ash, Elizabeth; "The Art of Visual Diplomacy", **State Magazine,** No. 464, January

2002   Osadchaja, Irina; "Old Birds Under One Roof", **Architecture and Design in the Baltics,** No. 5, Riga, Latvia, October; Color reproductions: *Heron,* 1995, and *Heron, Warbler and Milkweed,* 1991

"In the News: Artist and Their Art Go Abroad", **State Magazine,** No. 463, December; Color reproduction: *Heron, Warbler and Milkweed,* 1991

2000   Bailey, Susan; "Western Explorers Meet Explorations on Canvas and Film", **Seattle Wood River Journal,** August 2; 2000; Color reproduction: *Forest Site with River & Orchids,* 2000

Stasz, Meagan; "Painting Profile: Modern Landscape Painting", **Sun Valley Art,** Vol. 6, Nos. 8 & 9, February-March; Color reproductions: *Forest Site with Orchids & Wild Grass,* 2000 and *Forest Canopy & Botanicas,* 2000

1986   Cohrs, Timothy; "Hudson River Editions, Pelavin Editions-A Report Back from the Other World of Printmaking", **Arts Magazine,** November; Color reproduction: *Stag/Red Meander,* 1985

REVIEWS OF GROUP EXHIBITIONS

2020   O'Shaughnessy, Tracey; "Celebration of a Unique Singularity: Monoprint Show Featured", **REP/Republican American,** June 13

2001   Shaw, Kurt; "Pair of Shows Comment on Environmental Issues Facing Our Nation and the World", **Tribune,** Review, November 16

1988	Ahlander, Leslie Judd; "Sculpture is the focus of Gallery Show", **The Miami News,** June 3; Reproduction: *Standing Camel,* 1988
1985	Cecil, Sarah; "Group Show: Wolff Gallery", **ARTnews,** January
1983	Miro, Marsha; Review, **Detroit Free Press,** November
	Review, **Detroit News,** November
1981	Review, **Where Magazine,** August
1980	Larsen, Kay; "Reports from the Front", **The Village Voice,** Vol. 25, No. 7
	Rickey, Carrie; Review, **The Village Voice**

REVIEWS OF FINE ART PRINTS

2014	"Selected New Editions", **Art in Print,** March-April; Color reproduction: *Cliff Site with Red Heron,* monoprint, 2013
	"New Editions", **Journal of the Print World,** April/May/June; Color reproduction: *Amber Birds with Indigo Mountain,* 2013
2001	Szeto-Chan, Erin; Review, **In New York,** Eclectic Collector, July; Color reproduction: *Tiger Orchid/ Sri Lanka,* monoprint, 2001
1992	Marimo, Meri; Review, **Twenty-First Century Prints,** August; Color reproduction: *River Edge,* monoprint, 1990
1988	Review, **Print News: International Journal of Contemporary Prints,** Vol. 8, No. 2, Spring; Color reproduction: *Ragtime Hart,* monoprint,1985
1986	Beller, Tom; "Ancient Art Comes Alive" **West Side Spirit,** Arts & Entertainment, July 14; Color reproductions: *Leaping Brindled Stag,* 1984 and *Ragtime Hart,* 1984
1984	Cohen, Ronny; "New Editions", **ARTnews,** April; Color reproduction: *Dune Horse/Starry Night,* lithograph, 1984
	Review, **The Print Collectors Newsletter,** Vol. 15, No. 3, July-August; Color reproductions: *Claret Stag in Plum Field,* 1984 and *Leaping Brindled Stag,* 1984
1983	Review, **The Print Collectors Newsletter,** Vol. 14, No. 5; Color reproduction: *Dune Horse/Starry Night,* 1983

REPRODUCTIONS OF PAINTINGS IN PUBLICATIONS

2017 **International Journal of Visual Arts, Studies and Communication,** Volume 20; Number 20; publisher Dr. Shekhar Chandra Joshi, Almora, Uttarakhand, India; Front and back cover color reproductions: *Stag in Blue Field,* 2014, *Kali/ Black Madonna,* 1998 and *Valley of Flowers,* 2015

2015 Walsh, Mary; **Kinetiv: Highlights from the Polsinelli Art Collection;** Color reproduction: *Amber Birds with Indigo Mountain,* 2013

2010 Hayes, Linda; "Tall Order", **Luxe Magazine:** Interiors + Design Pacific Northwest Edition, Issue 1, Vol. 8, Winter; Color reproduction: *River Fragments Grey Bird,* 1990

2006 **The Lakeville Journal,** August 10; Reproduction: *Eurasian Steppe Horse,* 2004

2005 **The National Academies Press,** Trade Offerings; publisher Joseph Henry Press, Color reproduction: *Cranes, Warblers and Ironwood,* 2003

2005 **The National Academies Press,** New and Forthcoming Books, publisher Joseph Henry Press; Color reproduction: *Shore Site,* 2005

2002 Seely, Christopher; **Southern Voice,** October 11; Color reproduction: *Yellow Bird in Grey Field,* 2002

2000 **Idaho Mountain Express,** Arts & Events Sun Valley, August 2; Color reproduction: *Forest Site with Spotted Stag,* 2000

1999 **The Sciences Magazine,** Volume 39, No. 4, July/August; Color reproduction: *Pond Site,* 1999

1997 "Hodges Taylor Gallery is Moving", **Carolina Arts,** Vol. 1, No. 9; Color reproduction: *Red Spotted Horse,* 1997

Southern Accents, Charlotte; Color reproduction: *Red Horse/ Split,* 1997

1992 **Christian Science Monitor,** November 23; Color reproduction: *Heron Cove,* 1990

1991 **The Menniger Perspective,** Issue No. 3; Color reproduction: *Eastern Quarter,* 1991

1990 **Ms Magazine,** poster publication; Color reproduction: *Heron Cove,* 1990

1988 **The Pollock Krasner Foundation Annual Report;** Reproduction: *Strata,* 1984

Legacy Foundation; Color reproduction: *Good Medicine,* monoprint, 1996

1985 "The Ancestor that Wasn't", **The Sciences Magazine,** March/April; Color reproduction: *Back to Back,* 1984

1983 **The Newark Museum Annual Report,** Reproduction: *Bucks Country,* 1983

1980 **Maenad Magazine,** Reproduction: *Spotted Bison,* 1980

PUBLICATIONS AND CATALOGS

FINE ART PRINT PUBLICATIONS

Tandem Press, 2013
Pelavin Editions, Ltd, 1984-2008
Solo Press, 1983

BOOKS

2024 **Horses, Bison and Beasts of the Silk Routes:** Valentina DuBasky, Abingdon Square Publishing (2024). 23 color plates

2020 **Horned and Antlered Animals**: Valentina DuBasky, Abingdon Square Publishing (2024). 30 color plates

2019 **Singular & Serial: Contemporary Monotype and Monoprint** by Catherine Kernan and E. Ashley Rooney with Laura G. Einstein, and Janice C. Oresman, Schiffer Publishing. Color plates

EXHIBITION CATALOGS

2019 **United States Embassy Beijing: Art in Embassies Exhibition**, introduction by Ambassador Terry Branstad, Color reproductions: *Yellow Crane and Moon*, 2017, *Herons, Warblers and Reed Grass*, 2017, and *Riverbirds, Fossils and Reeds*, 2005

2017 **The Trace,** Lichtundfire Gallery, essay by Jonathan Goodman, Color reproduction: *Bison*

2016 **The Journey of the Red Horse:** Horse and Stag Paintings by Valentina DuBasky, Abingdon Square Publishing, Color reproductions: Cover and 13 color plates

2014 **Tandem Press: Fine Contemporary Prints 2014,** Color reproductions: Monotypes and lithograph by Valentina DuBasky, 15 color plates, centerfold, pages 15-23

2008 **From [Different] Horizons of Rockshelter** by Shoocongdej, Rasmi, Silpakorn University Press, Bangkok, Thailand; Color reproductions: 6 paintings from the Pang Mapha Highland Archaeology Project

2005 **Riverbirds and Rainforests,** National Academy of Sciences Gallery, introduction by J.D. Talasak and essay by Cynthia Nadelman, Color reproductions: 11 color plates

2003 **United States Embassy Panama: Art in Embassies Exhibition,** introduction by Ambassador Linda E Watt; Color reproductions: *Untitled,* 1998, *Shore Site,* 1991 and *Rainforest,* 1999

2002   **Art in Embassies Exhibition: Residence of the American Ambassador Riga,** introduction by Ambassador Brian E. and Marcia Carlson; Color reproductions: *Heron, Warbler and Milkweed,* 1991 (cover) and *Heron,* 1995

        Toxic Landscapes: Artists Examine the Environment, Puffin Foundation; Reproduction: *Tragic Harvest,* 1991, p20

2001   **Forest Orchids & Fossils;** Cheryl Pelavin Fine Art, essay by Gerrit Henry; Color reproductions: 9 color plates

1999   **Oil & Wax: Chapter & Verse;** Color Reproduction: *Spotted Horse,* 1999

1998   **American Artists at American Ambassador's Residence - Muscat, Sultanate of Oman,** introduction by Ambassador Frances D. Cook; Color Reproduction: *Heron Cove,* 1990, p14

1990   **Presswork: the Art of Women Printmakers**, essays by Eleanor Hartney and Trudy Hanson, Lang Publications; Color reproduction: *Heron Cove,* 1990

1987   **Rutgers Archives for Printmaking Studios, Catalog of Acquisitions, 1985-1987,** Jane Voorhees Zimmerli Art Museum, Rutgers University; Reproductions: *Red Stag Diptych,*1984, *Leaping Brindled Stag,* 1984, *Claret Stag in Plum Field,* 1984, *Small Stag Series,* 1984, and *Gray Stag/Ochre Field,* 1984

1985   **Intaglio Printing in the 1980's,** essay by Vivian Raynor; Jane Voorhees Zimmerli Art Museum

1984   **Surface Printing in the 1980's; Lithographs, Screenprints & Monoprints from the Rutgers Archives for Printmaking Studios,** Jane Voorhees Zimmerli Art Museum, Rutgers University; essay by Donna Gustafon, Reproduction: *Gray Stag/Ochre Field,* 1984;

1981   **The Working Process;** Color Reproduction: *Untitled,* 1981

        Mixed Bag, essay by Robert Browning, Alternative Museum, 1981; Reproduction: *Cumulus on the Mount,* 1981, p12

LIST OF PLATES

Spotted Horse in Claret Field (2016), oil on canvas, 22 x 30 inches	5
Amber Horse (2016), oil on canvas, 22 x 30 inches	7
Red Split Horse (2016), oil on canvas, 22 x 30 inches	9
Spotted Cloud Horse (2018), acrylic and marble dust on plaster and paper, 29.75 x 32 inches	11
Spotted Goat with Spiral Horns (2017), oil on paper, 22 x 28 inches	13
Cerulean and White Spotted Horse (2017), oil on paper, 22.5 x 30 inches	15
Spotted Goat with Amber Horns (2017), oil on paper, 22 x 30 inches	17
Red Horse with Bells (2016), oil on canvas, 22 x 30 inches	19
Bison (2017), mixed media on plaster and paper, 30.5 x 33 inches	21
Blue Antlered Stag in Rust Field (2017), oil on paper, 22.5 x 30 inches	23
White Spotted Horse (2017), oil on paper, 22.5 x 30 inches	25
Angkor Bison in Rose Field (2016), oil on paper, 22 x 30 inches	27
Winged Horse and Figures (2017), mixed media on plaster and paper, 30.5 x 33 inches	29
Grey Spotted Horse in Pink Field (2017), oil on canvas, 16 x 20 inches	31
Turning Stag with Rose Antlers (2020), oil on paper, 22 x 30 inches	33
Winged Amber Horse (2018), acrylic and marble dust on plaster and paper, 29.75 x 32 inches	35
Split Stag in Red Field (2018), oil on canvas, 24 x 20 inches	37
Dunhuang Horse (2009), watercolor and ink on paper, 6.25 x 8.75 inches	41
Markhor Goat with Spiral Horns (2009), watercolor and ink on paper, 4.5 x 9 inches	42
Recumbent Horse with Turning Head (2014), watercolor monotype with gouache, 12 x 9 inches	43
Leaping Deer and Tiger (2009), watercolor and ink on paper, 8.75 x 7 inches	44
Donkey (2009), watercolor and ink on paper, 7.5 x 5.5 inches	45
Goat (2009), watercolor and ink on paper, 7.5 x 5.5 inches	46

www.ingramcontent.com/pod-product-compliance
Lightning Source LLC
Chambersburg PA
CBHW051840210526
45473CB00005B/1956